Thomas Berger

Twayne's United States Authors Series

Warren French, Editor
University of Wales, Swansea

TUSAS 550

THOMAS BERGER
(1924-   )
Photograph by Jerry Bauer

Thomas Berger

By Brooks Landon

University of Iowa

Twayne Publishers
A Division of G.K. Hall & Co. • *Boston*

2/12 NONE LISTED 2
LAD TC
6/14 SAME

7/19 LAD 2

813.09 BERGER

Thomas Berger
Brooks Landon

Copyright 1989 by G.K. Hall & Co.
All rights reserved.
Published by Twayne Publishers
A Division of G.K. Hall & Co.
70 Lincoln Street
Boston, Massachusetts 02111

Copyediting supervised by Barbara Sutton
Book production by Patricia D'Agostino
Book design by Barbara Anderson

Typeset in 11 pt. Garamond
by Compositors Typesetters

Printed on permanent/durable acid-free paper
and bound in the United States of America

Library of Congress Cataloging-in-Publication Data
Landon, Brooks.
Thomas Berger / by Brooks Landon.
p.   cm. — (Twayne's United States authors series; TUSAS 550)
Bibliography: p.
Includes index.
ISBN 0-8057-7540-4 (alk. paper)
1. Berger, Thomas, 1924-   —Criticism and interpretation.
I. Title.   II. Series.
PS3552.E719Z78   1989
813'.54—dc19
                                                    88-37580
                                                    CIP

For Bren and Richard and Marie.
And for the two families that make most things possible.

Contents

About the Author

Brooks Landon received his B.A. from Centre College of Kentucky and, after serving in the U.S. Army, his M.A. and Ph.D. from the University of Texas at Austin. He is an associate professor in the Department of English at the University of Iowa, where he teaches courses in contemporary literature and science fiction film. His writing on American literature has appeared in the *Nation, American Literature, Philological Quarterly*, the *Iowa Review*, and *Studies in American Humor*. His writing on science fiction film has appeared in *Cinefantastique*, the *Mississippi Review*, and in numerous anthologies. He is currently completing *The Aesthetics of Ambivalence: The American Science Fiction Movie Examined* for Greenwood Press.

Preface

> If art is important, if civilization is important, the problem of style is important.
> —Remy de Gourmont, *Selected Writings*[1]

Worse than having a secret you cannot share is having one you cannot get enough people to listen to. For years Thomas Berger has been my secret, his novels a source of joy, amazement, puzzlement, and strength in my life. Berger's writing, more than that of any other novelist, raises for me the issues that seem most important, whether of language, of literature, or of experience itself. And for years I've struggled to explain my fascination to others—indeed, to make sense of it for myself. This book represents the desperation, and constitutes the culmination, of my efforts—it is the report of my study and an acknowledgment of its perhaps necessary incompleteness. Which is to say that I no longer can delude even myself into believing that this book is the final word in Berger criticism. I hope, however, it is a worthy start.

Berger's ever-growing number of devoted readers know how difficult a task it is to describe his writing. No single book stands much chance of charting the many delightful twistings and turnings of Thomas Berger's novels. Those fifteen books wear fifteen different masks, cutting across so many convenient critical categories and defying so many well-fed expectations that only the most general descriptions can introduce the neophyte to Berger's writing, celebrating as it does the diversity of novel forms, the complexities of language, the paradoxes of the human condition, and the possibilities of prose style. Perhaps the one thing on which critics agree is that Berger's talent is unique. The variety of Berger's novels, a range with no equal in contemporary American literature, underlines the precision of his craft, while distracting us from the steadiness and the seriousness of his purpose. And because Berger's central concerns are deeper and older than those associated with any particular culture in which his novels are set, they are particularly challenging to describe.

A recent example serves to introduce this perplexing characteristic. When Russel Wren, the relentlessly self-victimizing soft-boiled detective protagonist of Berger's eighth novel, *Who Is Teddy Villanova?*, reappears in *Nowhere*, Berger's thirteenth, he finds himself shanghaied (a term any Berger protagonist would stop to reflect upon) to the previously unheard-of kingdom of Saint Sebastian, a territory whose maps would be familiar to Swift, Jorge Luis Borges, or Vladimir Nabokov, but whose customs are so honestly and realistically drawn from human experience as to seem utterly fantastic to most readers. Among the initially odd-seeming practices Wren discovers in Saint Sebastian is the editing of the *Encyclopedia Sebastiana* by a group of scholars who initiate and revise its entries purely on the basis of personal whimsy. The entry under AIRPLANE, for example, reads:

The swiftest means of covering great distances in the shortest time. Its advantages over the bus, the train, and the various private vehicles are, in addition to speed, cleanliness, availability of toilets, and, strange as it might seem, according to statistics, safety; but it should be remembered that the normal passenger on an airplane never feels really secure. Most of us have our hearts in our mouths from the moment we take off until the landing is made, for although accidents might be rare statistically speaking, when one does happen, it's terrible, often resulting in hundreds of deaths.

When Wren dutifully questions the fairness of this procedure and suggests that an alternative might be to "seriously pursue the facts, the truth, in the various areas of human enterprise, and record them, it, as carefully, as objectively, as possible," one scholar observes, "That sounds like more work than we have stomach for," while another explains, "It's great fun to be totally irresponsible, whereas being careful about truth is a dreary way to live."[2]

Any introduction to the writing of Thomas Berger must start with such a passage representative of hundreds very like it throughout his novels. Of course the AIRPLANE entry sounds inappropriate, of course Russel Wren's perplexity sounds reasonable, and of course the scholars' response confirms and mocks our worst suspicions about any number of scholarly enterprises. But it is precisely because Thomas Berger *is* careful about "truth" that this exchange offers a crucial key to the understanding and interpretation of his fiction, and it is precisely because Berger is so determined by disposition to avoid the dreariness implicit in so many literary quests for truth that his novels form such a delightfully difficult challenge. At the heart of that challenge is the author's completely ironic vision, one that relies on ironizing as the one method through which "truth" may be rigorously pursued, instead of merely using it as a hedge against sincerity.

The reader who thinks Berger approves of Russel Wren's echoing the received idea that objectivity is the goal of referential writing is in for as big a surprise as is the reader who thinks Berger is mocking Saint Sebastian's scholars. Indeed, either reaction—or even the opposite stance, suspecting mockery in his presentation of Wren or approval in his presentation of the encyclopedists—distracts us from the starting and ending points of all

Berger's fiction: that truth, objectivity, knowledge, facts, the right, the good, and similar absolutes can be approached only through dialectic. And in Berger's canon, approach is all, and attainment is beyond the author's concern: being "careful about truth" may indeed be dreary, insofar as truth is equated with some grail-like goal, but as is clear to the readers of Berger's *Arthur Rex*, the grail is but a convenient justification for a search, the questing its own reward.

Zulfikar Ghose, one of Berger's best friends and a poet, novelist, and critic whose sensibility often parallels Berger's, has astutely written of the principle that organizes all of the quests for truth in Berger's novels. "The fantasy that precedes the knowledge of identity is invariably bizarre, but often the revelation of knowledge, both in art and in life, is so shockingly contradictory to the world of appearances that it seems to have been contrived by a fantastical imagination. It is not so. Berger has a phrase for it: it is the way reality operates."[3]

Operation is the key: motion, process, the give and take of living in time, the dialectical synthesis of opposing forces, whether people, ideas, or the words that form the raging sea of language in which people and ideas both must swim. A vital corollary to Berger's view of the way reality operates is his apparent conviction that only through a better understanding of the conflicts structuring the operation of reality—a search for truths—can personal freedom be found. And so thoroughgoing is this philosophy in Berger's writing that no one is spared, characters and readers alike. Just as Russel Wren must work through dialectical situations in even the most banal moments of his fictional life, Berger's reader must confront the stylistic dialectic inherent in his very presentation of Wren, as when the putative hard-boiled detective confounds our tough-guy expectations in *Who Is Teddy Villanova?* with his primly precise description of a ham-fisted punch: "He had struck me on the forehead, that helmet of protective bone, an impractical stroke even for such stout fingers as his, had he not turned his hand on edge and presented to my skull the resilient karate blade that swells out between the base of the smallest digit and the wrist: in his case, the size and consistency of the fleshy side of a loin of pork."[4]

Just as "the way reality operates"—actually operates, as opposed to the way it is said or thought to—is the constant subject of Berger's inquiry, the way his writing actually *operates*—as opposed to what might be expected of it, what it has been called or categorized as—is the constant focus of this study. My discussion starts with an overview of Berger's career, then turns to analysis of individual novels. Chapter 2 follows the progression of Berger's celebrated Reinhart series, *Crazy in Berlin, Reinhart in Love, Vital Parts,* and

Reinhart's Women, books that span most of his years as a novelist. As both the Reinhart series and the fact that *Who Is Teddy Villanova?* and *Nowhere* share Russel Wren as a protagonist suggest, the chronological order of Berger's novels is less important than their relationships, and so my grouping of the novels is conceptual, rather than chronological.

My third chapter examines Berger's best-known novel, *Little Big Man*, while chapter 4 turns to its legendary twin, *Arthur Rex*. In these two sweeping novels Berger takes on, respectively, the great American literary myth of the Old West and its mythic parallel and precursor, the Matter of Britain— the legend of King Arthur.

Chapter 5 covers Berger's most radical literary "subversions of good order," *Killing Time, Regiment of Women, Who Is Teddy Villanova?*, and its sequel, *Nowhere*. Chapter 6 explores Berger's longstanding fascination with the relationship between victims and victimizers, a relationship always near the center of *Being Invisible, Sneaky People, The Feud, Neighbors,* and *The Houseguest*. My final chapter offers an overview of the major constants in Berger's style, his celebrations of novel forms, his preoccupation with the theme of language, and the importance of Nietzsche in his writing.

In-text page references are to the most recent editions cited in the bibliography, quotations from Berger's letters to me are identified by parenthetical dates in the text.

One final note on my manner of proceeding is in order. Nothing in Berger's writing is more important—to author and reader alike—than the specificity of its language. For Berger, as much as for Henry James, the style of his prose surfaces offers one sure index to his deeper concerns as a novelist. For this reason, I frequently quote the language of the novels themselves. The stylistic core of Berger's genius and the essence of his accomplishment remain ever beyond the crudity of paraphrase and summary. To read and understand the novels of Thomas Berger, one must look *at*, as well as through, his sentences: Accept no substitutes!

Brooks Landon

University of Iowa

Acknowledgments

The problem is that I know exactly where to start and how long it would take me to recognize properly the people who made this book not just possible, but inevitable—and I'll never get the job done right. Zulfikar Ghose got me started on this study about a dozen years ago, although neither of us knew it then, and my debt to him is greater now than he can possibly realize. Reading Thomas Berger has been the great love of my intellectual life; corresponding with him has been a delight and an education. I am grateful to him for permission to quote both from his novels and from our correspondence. Assistance from the University of Iowa has included summer fellowships and a semester of developmental leave. My gratitude for the wonderful patience and support provided by Jay Semel and Lorna Olson at University House, University of Iowa, is simply beyond measure.

Portions of this study have appeared in somewhat different form in the *Nation, Philological Quarterly,* and *Studies in American Humor.* Passages from Thomas Berger's *Crazy in Berlin, Reinhart in Love, Little Big Man, Killing Time, Vital Parts, Regiment of Women, Sneaky People, Who Is Teddy Villanova?, Arthur Rex, Neighbors, Reinhart's Women, The Feud,* and *Nowhere* are reprinted by arrangement with Delacorte Press. Passages from Berger's *Being Invisible* and *The Houseguest* are reprinted by permission of Little, Brown & Co.

Chronology

Goes to London for latter part of year, then returns to Gramercy Park, where he resides until late in 1974.

1970   *Vital Parts.* Play *Other People* performed 1–11 July at Berkshire Theatre Festival. Arthur Penn's film of *Little Big Man.*

1971–1972   Collaborates with Milos Forman on film script of *Vital Parts,* but project is eventually abandoned.

1972–1973   Film columnist for *Esquire.*

1973   *Regiment of Women.*

1973–1974   Gives readings at many colleges and in November is writer in residence, University of Kansas.

1974–1976   Lives at Bridgehampton, Long Island.

1975   *Sneaky People.*

1975–1976   Distinguished visiting professor, Southampton College.

1976–1979   Lives on Mount Desert Island in Maine.

1977   *Who Is Teddy Villanova?.*

1978   *Arthur Rex.*

1979   Returns to live on the Hudson River outside New York.

1980   *Neighbors.*

1981   *Reinhart's Women.* Regents' lecturer, University of California at Davis, in November. Film of *Neighbors* released.

1981–1982   Visiting lecturer at Yale.

1983   *The Feud.*

1984   Judges select *The Feud* for the 1984 Pulitzer Prize; selection overruled in favor of William Kennedy's *Ironweed* by the Pulitzer administrative committee.

1985   *Nowhere.*

1986   Given honorary doctor of letters degree by Long Island University.

1987   *Being Invisible.*

1988   *The Houseguest.*

Chapter One

A Radical Sensibility

A Career of Quiet Dazzle

For over twenty-five years Thomas Berger has been one of America's most productive and most enigmatic literary figures. Author of fifteen novels, Berger easily ranks among the most accomplished novelists since the end of World War II, and his writing seems sure to earn him a lasting place in American letters. His novels have established him as not only one of our most energetic writers but also one of the most unpredictable, since no two of his books seem, at first glance, to have much in common. The fact that each of his books seems to follow a different genre convention is further complicated by the fact that no established genres prepare his readers for what his novels quickly become. Having read *Little Big Man*, readers and critics alike find it quite difficult to understand how *Regiment of Women* could come from the same writer. And the task is almost as difficult with any two of Berger's novels: little in *Arthur Rex* prepares us for *Neighbors*, little in *Neighbors* prepares us for *Reinhart's Women*, and for that matter, no two books in the Reinhart series seem much alike. Over a decade ago, Richard Schickel called Berger "one of the most radical sensibilities now writing novels in this country," and any careful examination of Berger's novels more than confirms the wisdom of Schickel's claim.[1] One of the great achievements, as well as part of the difficulty, of Berger's novels is that they consistently measure up to F. Scott Fitzgerald's famed "test of a first-rate intelligence." Both his novels, considered individually and collectively, and many of the characters in those novels reveal Berger's ability to hold two—and sometimes more than two—"opposed ideas in the mind, at the same time, and still retain the ability to function." And it is in the complicated dialectic that emerges from these oppositions that the "radical" nature of Berger's sensibility most clearly reveals itself.

Berger's range, not to mention the depth of his concerns, has discouraged more than superficial consideration of his work. The writer who resists conventional pigeonholing is the bane of reviewers and surveyors alike: without being able to locate a given writer within the context of a recognizable genre, philosophy, or movement, or without being able to compare the writer with other well-known writers, the critic must do quite a bit of work to describe, much less analyze, the singular writer. Since Berger's "celebrations" of these classic genres end up in ways quite beyond genre expectations, and since perhaps the only contemporary writer with whom Berger can be profitably compared, Vladimir Nabokov, is also highly resistant to generalization, reviewers have usually opted to focus on a single Berger novel, declining the challenge of relating it to the rest of his canon, or, indeed, of seeing that his seemingly disparate novels are related by more than the accident of authorship.

While Berger's work has been prominently reviewed, he has had no real critics. Critical surveys of the contemporary American novel invariably mention him—usually in the company of Joseph Heller, J. P. Donleavy, William Gass, John Barth, or Thomas Pynchon—but mention is all that he receives. Much more is involved here, however, than the by-now almost ritual noting of critical vagary: Berger's longstanding critical invisibility speaks to the nature of his writing and not to its quality. Ultimately, to understand why Berger has been excluded from critical surveys of contemporary fiction is to begin to understand the singularity of Berger's novels. Brutally simplified, that singularity comes from writing that is in many ways nonrational while in no way fashionably unreadable.

Too subtly experimental to fit the mainstream of postwar American fiction, Berger's novels are also too familiar-seeming to fit the emerging canon of postmodernism. Shimmering somewhere between the narrow beam of literary realism and the kaleidoscopic flashes of metafiction is the steady flame of Berger's craft. "Midfiction," Alan Wilde has called it, fiction that "questions a traditional authorial center and power," while at the same time preserving "a referential, if not a representational function. Less spectacular but not for that reason less authentically experimental, it strenuously interrogates the world without foreclosing all knowledge of it and unsettles rather than topples our certainties and presuppositions by way of parody and other recyclings of fictional, cultural, even metaphysical givens."[2]

Although not concerned specifically with Berger or any other single author, Richard Ohmann has proposed a number of criteria that seem to distinguish postwar canonical fiction; his study, as distressing as it is persuasive, suggests a number of economic and ideological reasons why Berger's novels have not enjoyed the reception given works such as *Franny and Zooey, One Flew over the Cuckoo's Nest, The Bell Jar, Herzog, Portnoy's Complaint,* or Updike's Rabbit novels. Ohmann argues that "*the* story of the postwar period" characteristically charts "the project of happy selfhood," a search for personal fulfillment in which the absurdities and contradictions of society are transformed "into a dynamic of personal crisis."[3] Socially induced neurosis is the problem, and recovery is always problematic, in these "narratives of illness." Small wonder that Berger, a writer not at all ready to assume that unhappiness is evil or even relevant in the broader scheme of existence, has not been embraced by a literary establishment obsessed with "the project of happy selfhood." One of Berger's most astute critics and champions, Richard Schickel, arrived at much the same conclusion, via a slightly different route, in 1970, when he ascribed to Berger another unique trait: "In short, he accepts free enterprise, spiritual as well as economic, as the basis of our society, probably of Western civilization as well. He thinks it immutable—man being the fallen and greedy creature he is—and for all the difficulties it presents, the only viable basis on which to organize self and society. This is not calculated to win him the affection of the literary community, which has been, these many years, committed to quite another vision."[4]

What his novels affirm again and again, Berger has spelled out in a letter to Zulfikar Ghose, recalling a conversation with Arthur Koestler in which Koestler admitted he could not help trying to save the world:

He said this wryly, of course, and then asked me whether I felt the same urge. I said no, that I wouldn't walk across the street to save the world, because I did not see it as a problem to which there was a solution. . . . Existence seems to me to be simply *there*. It is certainly basically painful, but the true pain, beneath the inconveniences that *can* be dealt with, is not the kind of thing that can be eradicated by scientists or economists or politicians or mass religious movements; although to individuals involved in these, life may be more gratifying than it would be without a cause.[5]

Citing his belief in a "fundamental reciprocity, which maintains the principle of constant damage in the universe," Berger concluded simply that he did "not see life as responsive to any 'cure.'" Rejecting as chimerical the notion of a "cure" to life's problems, Berger has also rejected the dominant model of canonical postwar fiction: his characters are rarely truly happy, but their unhappiness should not be mistaken for disease. Carlo Reinhart may indeed be technically "crazy" in Berlin, Jack Crabb may be uncomfortably cognizant of the fact that madness seems to run in his family, and Joe Detweiler is in fact a psychopathic murderer, but in Berger's hands their lives can never be reduced to neurosis, their quests never limited to something so shallow as "happy selfhood." The distinction may seem a fine one, but it nevertheless suggests at once the reason why a critic like Schickel would sense in Berger's writing "the most radical sensibility of any writer now writing in America," as well as why that sensibility has been so guardedly received.

For years it was fashionable to decry the fact that Berger had received neither the critical attention nor the popular acclaim his novels merited.
Schickel, always one of Berger's ablest critics, expressed the sad conviction in
1970 that "Thomas Berger will never achieve the recognition he deserves."[6]
Over a decade later, Thomas R. Edwards concluded his review of *Neighbors*
with a more militant charge that the failure to read and discuss Berger's work
is "a national disgrace."[7] The years between those comments, however, saw
Berger's *Little Big Man* become an immensely popular film as well as a
widely read and taught literary classic, and then they saw *Who Is Teddy
Villanova?* outsell *Little Big Man*. Berger's *Arthur Rex* was hailed as "the
Arthur story for our time," and Berger's eighth, ninth, and tenth novels (*Who
Is Teddy Villanova?, Arthur Rex,* and *Neighbors*) all proved to be both popular and critical successes. Indeed, only a last-minute administrative decision
to bypass the first choice of the committee of judges denied Berger's twelfth
novel, *The Feud*, a Pulitzer Prize in 1984. So, while it is safe to say that
Berger's distinctive talents have not yet been systematically studied, it is no
longer the case that they have gone unrecognized and unapplauded.

The Gift of Style

That Berger has not received more detailed study is a comment on the nature of his writing as much as, or more than, on its quality. Like many of his
main characters, Berger simply does not seem to fit existing critical
categories—or, more perversely, he seems to fit several antithetical ones at
once. His fiction swells with paradoxes, seeming to embrace what it exposes
as delusion, celebrating what it seems to parody, absolutely refusing to subscribe to any codified philosophy, whether romantic, existentialist, or
absurdist. His prose style challenges the reader with precise but often elaborate or serpentine sentences, and those sentences are as full of surprises as are
Berger's characters and plots. If we can be sure of only one thing in his writing, it is that expectations are meant to be disproved. To this end, Berger tries
to make of each novel an "independent existence," an alternative reality he
hopes the reader will approach "without the luggage of received ideas, *a
priori*–assumptions, sociopolitical axes to grind, or feeble moralities in search
of support" (8 November 1976). Berger has persisted in the writing of novels
that are aggressively intelligent and consistently resistant to the twin senti-
mentalities of idealism and despair. His career has been a delightfully eccen-
tric refusal to cook what D. H. Lawrence once called "the awful pudding of
One Identity," and one of the consequences of this refusal has been that the
identity of Berger's style has remained more a matter for passing comment

than for explanation. Something of the difficulty of describing that underlying style may be seen in Leonard Michaels's review of *Who Is Teddy Villanova?* for the *New York Times Book Review*. After praising Berger's style as "educated, complicated, graceful, silly, destructive in spirit," Michaels could only conclude that "Berger's style is like itself insofar as it is like other styles."[8]

The underlying thesis of this book, however, is that the interpretation of Berger's novels *is* the study of his style and that the discussion of meaning really centers on the ways in which a reader experiences his writing. As a critical stance, such a reader-oriented aesthetics is by now well known, but apart from being theoretically justifiable, this approach is mandated by the specific nature of Berger's writing. When Berger suggests that only the "selfish" reader will get the most out of his work, he explicitly spells out what his novels implicitly demand: far from encouraging readers to "lose" themselves in fiction, the novels challenge their readers to become conscious of themselves in the act of reading.[9]

A Life Amused and Concealed by Language

Only the most oblique and ultimately insignificant connections can be drawn between the circumstances of Berger's life and the particulars of his fiction. Burroughs Mitchell, Berger's first editor at Scribners, recalls that Berger and his wife lived near him in the mid-1950s, and he describes the novelist as "a big, smiling man with a mild and cheerful manner that I think it would be correct to call misleading."[10] Mitchell's bemused caveat that "the fruitless entertainment of trying to perceive the nature of a man's writing from his manner would prove particularly futile with Tom Berger" reverses the normal direction of critical inquiry, but it is significant that in a critical community historically fascinated with building even the flimsiest of bridges from the writer's fiction to the writer's life, only one scholar has attempted to equate Berger's sensibility with that of his most autobiographical-seeming character, Carlo Reinhart. And that effort by Alan Wilde, while revealing a number of fine insights into Berger's novels, makes its sophisticated case only for phenomenological *parallels* between author and character—doing so, in places, at the expense of disregarding what can be advanced as contradictory evidence both in the Reinhart novels and in Berger's other fiction.[11]

In 1987 the *New York Times Book Review* asked a number of authors, including Berger, "Which of the characters you have created has had the greatest effect on your own life?" Berger's response, which I find compelling, deserves our attention.

I began the writing of my first novel with the assumption that its principal character should be myself under a pseudonym, and for years (*Crazy in Berlin* took four)
I tried to fashion a marionette in my own image. But I got no farther than the first
page until I came to understand that fiction must never be confused with that existence through which I make my daily slog—that what I required by way of a hero
was almost anybody but myself. At that point a character named Reinhart appro-
priated the role: a better man than I, generous where I am mean, kinder, braver, not
even afraid to be taken for a fool—unlike me, in my novelist's cap and bells! I have
been a voyeur of this essential fellow through three subsequent narratives. Whatever I am, Reinhart has the peculiar ability to dramatize what I am *not*. Perhaps I
shall finally have the wit to recognize that I am more his creation than he has ever
been mine.[12]

Nevertheless, a brief summary of Berger's background may be of interest,
particularly since his desire for privacy has given him something of a reputation as a recluse. Even that is misleading, Michael Malone has wryly observed, explaining, "While it is true that he takes no part in the New York
flashdance (having concluded long ago that it is our sad fate to live in an age
when 'the Philistines *are* the intelligentsia'), he is by no means a social misan-
thrope, but rather as warm, ebullient, and charming a hermit as anyone is
likely to meet." Malone astutely specifies, "We are unlikely, however, to meet
him on a talk show," since "Berger is a writer (a private act), not a Writer (a
public art), nor an Author (a critical cult)."[13]

As a man, as well as a writer, Berger both invites and defies description. In
his mid-sixties, he is a big man whose shaved head draws attention to pene-
trating eyes under eyebrows he once described as "arched in perpetual curiosity." Recent jacket photos invariably show him wearing a dark turtleneck.
The overall effect manages to be at once faintly monkish and vaguely Charles
Adamsish—a distinct but indecipherable suggestion of what the Czech film
director Milos Forman affectionately called Berger's "veerrdness."

Berger was born in Cincinnati, Ohio, in 1924 and grew up in the nearby
suburban community of Lockland, where he attended the same public
school from kindergarten through high school. His father was the school's
business manager. Berger notes of his childhood, "Very early in life, I discovered that for me reality was too often either dull or obnoxious, and while I did
play all the popular games that employ a ball, lower hooks into the water,
and, especially fire guns, I preferred the pleasure of the imagination to those
of experience, and I read incessantly."[14]

Of his reading interests as a boy, Berger has fondly mentioned his "own
boyhood King Arthur . . . the work of one Elizabeth Lodor Merchant, Head

of the Department of English, William Penn High School, Philadelphia, Penna," a gift from his father at Christmas 1931 (19 July 1977). Terming it "almost the only worthwhile reference of that sort to be found in a review of any book of mine" (but then also pointing out the kind of potential influence literary criticism usually is blind to), Berger wrote of a reference to Thorne Smith in a Walter Clemons review of *Regiment of Women*: "Here's something amusing: of course I did not have *Turnabout* in the front of my mind while writing ROW, but during the latter years of high school and the early Army time, Thorne Smith was my favorite writer, and I did read and enjoy *Turnabout*" (21 June 1979). When in high school, Berger worked part-time in a branch of the Cincinnati Public Library, and he also did library work when he was in college, experience that would later help him secure his first job in New York City.

In a letter to Zulfikar Ghose, who has been one of Berger's closest friends since they met in England in 1963 (Ghose had been the anonymous reviewer of *Reinhart in Love* for the *Times Literary Supplement*), Berger has explained that "the one art to which I was at all exposed as a child was music," citing both the influence of his mother and that of Cincinnati's status as "a provincial music center, with a symphony orchestra, two colleges of music, and a summer opera season," but characteristically concluding that "it was therefore predictable that I should be utterly unmusical."[15]

In 1981 Berger reported, of his return to his hometown of Lockland (population now under 5,000) for the fortieth reunion of his 1941 high school graduation class:

My classmates were most of them working-class people. Only three or four of us ever went to college. Not many of them, I should think, have ever read a book. An old local pal of mine told me that he was looking through the yearbooks of the past and that I was the only person, of all those faces throughout all the years of that high school, who became "famous." I was touched, but I also reflected silently that I am probably also the only one who ever: ate zucchini, had a self-acknowledged homosexual as nonerotic friend, or had four different permanent addresses in five years—to name only a few of my real distinctions. (7 June 1981)

The circumstances of Berger's childhood do not seem to have had much of a direct influence on his fiction (certainly little, if anything, in his writing could be termed autobiographical in any strict sense), but the *sounds* of his childhood—the speech he grew up listening to—have exercised an influence little short of profound. *Sneaky People, The Feud,* and *Reinhart in Love* were generated as much from his fascination with the language of his childhood as from conventional concerns with plot, theme, or story. While writing *The Feud*, Berger reported, "I'm having a splendid time recreating the speech I heard when a child" (28 Jan 1982), and he has identified *Sneaky People* as "my tribute to the American language of 1939—to be philologically precise, that of the lower-middle class in the eastern Middle West, on which I am an authority as on nothing else."[16] More recently he explained: "I have all my life listened to the radio regularly, beginning in its golden age, the 1930's. And I don't have to remind you of my interest in sound, particularly that of human speech. In fact a good many of my sentences take their pretext from the sound of a certain word" (23 May 1979). Readers familiar with the trademark deadpan outrageousness of the radio duo of Bob and Ray may also find echoes of their style in Berger's writing. He acknowledges that he has long been a fan of their brilliant humor, terming them "masters of American dialogue" and concluding, "I should say that it is very likely they have been an important influence on me" (24 September 1987).

Disenchanted after a short bout with college, Berger enlisted in the army and served from 1943 to 1946, his experiences giving him some of the background for his first novel, *Crazy in Berlin*. In 1948 he received his B.A. at the University of Cincinnati, and was a graduate student in English at Columbia in the school year 1950–51. There he completed course work for an M.A. including a class with Lionel Trilling, and began a thesis on George Orwell, which he never completed. While it would be unwise to overestimate Trilling's influence on Berger's writing, it is important to note that many of Berger's statements about his fiction and many aspects of the fiction itself parallel Trilling's well-known beliefs, particularly as represented in his essay "The Meaning of a Literary Idea."[17] While Berger recalls that as a student in Trilling's famous course in modern American literature he "worshiped Trilling . . . and was much taken with his sort of sociocultural criticism" (28 January 1979), he downplays suggestion of lasting impact: "Make of Trilling's influence what you will. I don't see much of it in my fiction, in which I think my influences are other literary artists, not critics, and yes, the movies and TV" (11 June 1987). From academic graduate study, Berger turned his attention to the writers workshop at the New School for Social Research. At the New School, Berger "studied classical Greek and philosophy for a while with refugee professors from the great universities of Germany, who had fled Hitler" (11 June 1987). Called "the University in Exile," this special faculty can only have helped shape Berger's lifelong fascination with the parameters of freedom and victimization. In the New School writers workshop, Berger's fellow students included William Styron, Jack Kerouac, and Mario Puzo. Since 1950 Berger has been married to Jeanne Redpath, an artist he met at the New School. Under the aegis of workshop director Charles Glicksberg, Berger, who explains he had always thought of himself as a writer, began to write short stories:

I produced one story a week for three months, most of them melancholy in tone, maudlin in spirit, and simple of mind, Hemingway then being my model. Graduating in time to the influence of Faulkner, I published a thing or two of little merit during the next five years in "little" magazines, but I didn't begin my first novel and develop my own style, such as it is—and little did I know that it would be different in each successive novel—until I was within a few months of my thirtieth birthday.[18]

On another occasion, Berger considered other possible influences, emphasizing that most of his models are from the antique:

As to literary ancestors, at the beginning, with the first two Reinharts and perhaps LBM as well, I thought of myself as being in the vein of Smollett and Fielding (with *Don Quixote* before them), which comes along to Dickens, but then I always liked most those elements in Dickens which appealed to Dostoievsky, Proust, and Kafka, and those are the non-Smollettian properties, I should say. The humorous criticism of society has never been my purpose and I don't consider myself a satirist. I can't identify my ancestors until I determine what it is that I do. (28 January 1979)

"Dependency of Day and Night," published in the Spring 1952 *Western Review*, confirms the accuracy of this self-assessment, although the fact that Berger's protagonist—perhaps a prefiguration of Reinhart—languishes in the dermatitis section of an army hospital suggests that the Hemingway influence was even then heavily tempered by Berger's sense of irony.

Of his short fiction Berger is distinctly unenamored. As he has explained, "the marathon is my event, and not the hundred-yard dash":

My gift is not seen at advantage in short works of fiction. (Nor do I usually read short stories with much pleasure.) Perhaps this is because I do not have much room in a story to create my alternative reality—and I am not unusually eloquent as a mere commentator on the reality I must, being human, share with everyone else. To put it another way, in the novel I have before me the possibility of being Alexander or Caesar—or Genghis Khan: there is a land of some magnitude to conquer. But a story seems a kind of Liechtenstein or San Marino: what does one have when he has assaulted and taken it? A trade in postage stamps. (23 August 1977)

Despite this preference, Berger's short fiction has appeared in magazines ranging from the *Saturday Evening Post* to *Playboy* and *North American Re-*

view. He has also written numerous reviews and short satirical pieces for *Esquire,* where he also wrote a film column from 1972 to 1973. Berger has also written three plays, all unpublished, but one of which, *Other People,* was produced in 1970 at the Berkshire Theatre Festival in Massachusetts. A wickedly funny Berger radio play, *At the Dentist's,* was produced by Vermont Public Radio in 1981.

From 1948 through 1951, Berger supported his writing by working as a librarian at the Rand School of Social Science. Berger has explained that he responded to an ad in the NY Times "for a librarian at a private library with a specialized collection":

The job turned out to be at a little institution near Union Square, the old rallying place for radicals, called The Rand School of Social Science. This school was the creation of American Socialists around the turn of the century, and its first purpose was to provide immigrants with a political education. The founders, and the immigrants, were predominantly Jewish, and their principal leader was the Russian- or Polish-born Jew, Morris Hillquit, an impressive man and one of the important forces in the history of socialism in America. (15 September 1986)

One cannot read the issues of the *Institute of Social Studies Bulletin,* in which some of Berger's early book reviews appeared, without realizing that his work at the Rand School immersed him in an exciting, intellectually and ideologically charged environment, quite a break, no doubt, from earlier life with Protestant, "right-wing Ohio Republican" parents, when Berger had himself been completely uninterested in politics. Even in those early reviews, however, Berger's interest lay clearly in ideas rather than in ideologies, a distinction rigorously maintained throughout his writing and reflected in his further comment on the Rand School:

The library there consisted mainly of political books, though the concept from which the school was created did not seek to separate politics from culture—here you see that which distinguishes the Jews from all other ethnic groups in history: not, as the anti-Semites would have it, an unusual interest in money (which in fact is truer of everybody else), but rather a consistent preoccupation with the life of the mind. Thus even in the days of its flourishing, the Rand School offered as many adult-education courses in literature and the other liberal arts as those in which politics was the focus. (15 September 1986)

From 1951 to 1952, he was a staff member of the *New York Times Index,* and in the following year he was a copy editor for *Popular Science Monthly.* During the early 1950s, Berger wrote a number of reviews, many of which were for *New Leader* and the *Institute of Social Studies Bulletin*. Of particular note are those of Orwell's *Shooting an Elephant*, Koestler's *Age of Longing*, and Arendt's *Origins of Totalitarianism* in *Intro*, and those of *A Woman in Berlin* and Poliakov's *Harvest of Hate* in the *Socialist Call*. In the former three, Berger discusses the limitations, opportunities, and responsibilities of the ideological novel, while in the latter two can be found part of the likely background for his first novel, *Crazy in Berlin*. These early reviews offer little promise of Berger's subsequent prose style, nor do they more than hint at the complicated sensibility seen in his novels. Indeed, they suggest nothing so much as the kind of orthodox liberalism Berger now dismisses as "social meliorism."

Having lived in New York City from 1948 to 1953, Berger spent the next twelve years "in a little village on the Hudson River." He moved to London in 1965 and stayed there for a year. From London he moved to the beach at Malibu, California, for six months, then to another village on the Hudson for a year, before returning to London for the latter half of 1967. For the next seven and a half years, Berger again lived in New York City, followed by a year in the Hamptons on Long Island. He then moved to Mount Desert Island in Maine, staying there from 1976 through 1979, before moving to his present location, once more on the Hudson riverbank. "New York is a terrible place," Berger resignedly noted in 1977, "yet I am totally isolated when I am anywhere else in this country" (26 December 1977).

Until 1964 and the publication of his third novel, *Little Big Man*, Berger did freelance editing to supplement the income from his writing. That writing won a Dial fellowship in 1962, the Western Heritage Award in 1965, and the Rosenthal Award that same year. For the first semester of the 1981-82 school year, Berger was visiting lecturer at Yale. In 1983 Berger declined an appointment to the American Institute of Arts and Letters.

Little interested in teaching, lecturing, or participating in the literary community, Berger is first and last a novelist. "I never take a vacation," he has written, "because what would it be from? I became a novelist many years ago so that I might live in a continuum of make-believe in which there are no weekends and, more importantly, no Monday mornings" (6 September 1977). More recently, he concluded a written interview with Richard Schickel with a succinct personal credo. "I should like the reader to be aware that a book of mine is written in the English language, which I love with all my heart and write to the best of my ability and with the most honorable of intentions—which is to say, I am peddling no quackery, masking no intent to tyrannize, and asking nobody's pity. (I suspect that I am trying to save my own soul, but that's nobody else's business.)"[19]

Chapter Two
The Reinhart Series:
Crazy in Berlin,
Reinhart in Love, Vital Parts,
and *Reinhart's Women*

"It ought to begin to occur to you that life is just a collection of stories from all points of self-interest" (243). This excellent advice comes from Carlo Reinhart's shrewish but devastatingly pragmatic ex-wife, Genevieve, and, as is true of most good advice received by a character in a Thomas Berger novel, has no effect. There are some truths beyond the ken of even the enlightened and triumphant Reinhart of *Reinhart's Women,* Berger's eleventh novel, the most recent of the four novels that compose his celebrated Reinhart series. Taking four distinct forms and sharing only the developing sensibility of Carlo Reinhart, these novels, *Crazy in Berlin* (1958), *Reinhart in Love* (1962), *Vital Parts* (1970), and *Reinhart's Women* (1981), constitute one of the most significant accomplishments in postwar American literature. Even before the addition of *Reinhart's Women,* R. V. Cassill aptly described this series as a literary Moby-Dick whose "ambiguous carcass is so imposing and looms so enticingly amid the deep waters of the recent past that there is really no choice for the serious reader except to go after it with Ahab's passion."[1]

And it is characteristic of this series that Berger leaves to Genevieve, one of Reinhart's most effective nemeses, the opportunity to spell out one of the central assumptions of the Reinhart books, combining as it does Berger's constant theme, language, with his predominant technique, irony. Of course theme and technique are really one and the same in a Berger novel, particularly since the difference between word and object, between language and reality, gives rise to the fundamental irony that all of his novels explore. Understood by one of Reinhart's companions as "the only weapon whose victories were won exclusively from its wielder," irony strikes the Reinhart of *Crazy in Berlin* as "that means to confront the ideal with the actual and not go mad, that whip which produced the pain that hurts-so-good, so that in the measure to which it hurt it was also funny" (247). Able to understand the mechanism of irony only when its working is to his disadvantage, Reinhart is at once Berger's most ironic hero and most ironic victim.

Crazy in Berlin started Reinhart, "a stumbling American Odysseus," on what Berger has termed "his long career of indestructibility."[2] The other novels in the series follow Reinhart as he grows older and, ultimately, wiser. Summed up by one critic as "a clowning knight errant, pure of heart—that is, a custodian of our conscience and of our incongruities," Reinhart is an incurable idealist who really has no faith in idealism.[3] Driven by a profound respect for the moral dimension of any human action, he cannot find a moral code rigorous enough to command his allegiance. As Douglas Hughes put it, Reinhart's dilemma is that of "the confused but faithful modern humanist who senses that traditional values can no longer find philosophical justification, that there are *no* absolutes, but who remains loyal to these values in the name of decency and civilization."[4] Although moral codes fascinate Reinhart, he can rarely untangle their relations to power, and he usually understands only enough from each code to make him feel guilty. "You are the Mahatma Gandhi to my British Empire," he admits to his father, "I see your strength but don't get the moral behind it" (42).

Complexity, Reinhart's essence, is also his nemesis: he can always see both sides to every argument and feel responsibility for any injustice, and though he realizes that "true freedom is found only by being consistent with oneself," he has a devil of a time figuring out how to do this, particularly in the novels before *Reinhart's Women*. His problem is spelled out in *Reinhart in Love*: "His quest, of course, remained: freedom. And the way to it was tortuous because as yet he could not define the nature of his captivity, let alone identify the chief warden, though naturally he knew as well as anybody that we are our own jailors" (172). The freedom that Reinhart seeks is essentially a consistent rationale for his unimpressive, awkward, but indomitable individuality. Combining the features of "a big bland baseball bat" with those of "an avatar of Job the beloved of a sadistic God," Reinhart can never shake the suspicion that he does not fit anywhere, but is nonetheless responsible for the general muddle that surrounds and usually engulfs him. An emotional liberal, Reinhart nevertheless believes in the "fundamental immorality of sympathy." A key symptom of his time in the psycho ward at the end of *Crazy in Berlin* is his conviction—which recurs throughout his life—that "his purpose on earth was to rectify life's dirty deals." While he recognizes the folly in this view, his generosity of spirit inevitably betrays him: whether voiced or implied, whether by friend or by enemy, "Don't let me down" is the one bugle call Reinhart can never resist—at least in the books before *Reinhart's Women*.

Yet Reinhart is as ill-suited for despair as he is for success. Although reminded by a successful acquaintance that he is "redundant in the logistics of life," he can never really be disillusioned, even though his dreams steadily fall prey to the practical opportunism of those around him. No match for a mother who can tell him, "if I ever thought you had truck with Filth, I'd slip you strychnine" (RIL, 114), or a shrewish wife who advises him, "if you're going to be an ass-kisser, then you ought to at least kiss the asses of winners" (RW, 245), Reinhart can still recognize the distinction between his secular search for a Holy Grail and the social meliorism that passes for idealism. He vaguely realizes that he is trapped between the Scylla and Charybdis of belief, but like all of Berger's characters, Reinhart never gives up: an indomitable toughness underlies his numerous weaknesses, and whatever the situation, he always muddles through, scarred but undaunted.

Reinhart's Role in the Berger Canon

It is particularly important to begin the consideration of the Reinhart books with the reminder that Berger's concern is rarely with society (other than as a necessary proving ground for individualism), because among the author's fifteen novels, these four seem on their surfaces most like conventional, sociologically centered investigations of society and ideology. Berger acknowledges the singular features of these novels: "The Reinhart books don't really fit into the 'celebratory' sequence: they are as near as I can come to the standard novel-as-slice-of-life. I do one now and again to keep in touch with reality, for my connections to society get ever feebler" (7 December 1979).

The temptation to overstate Berger's connections to Reinhart is understandable, as character and author do have in common some biographical features, including birthdate (1924), birthplace (Ohio), ethnic background (German-American), and army service (with the first occupation troops in Berlin). "Berger, like Reinhart," Gerald Weales has observed, "is concerned with the dangerous uncertainty of human relationships, familial, sexual, collegial, with the problem of identity, with the slipperiness of truth, with the inefficacy of language, with the authoritarianism of self-righteous idealism, with aging and death."[5] But then who among us is not? Weales only notes the above correspondences in the service of his more important argument that "whatever autobiographical elements, statistical and spiritual, go into the Reinhart novels, the creator and the created are not one," a conclusion obvious to readers who are familiar with Berger's non-Reinhart novels.[6] Having once termed himself "Reinhart's father," Berger has recently suggested:

"Whatever I am, Reinhart has the peculiar ability to dramatize what I am *not*. Perhaps I shall finally have the wit to recognize that I am more his creation than he has ever been mine."[7] Nevertheless, Berger does acknowledge one autobiographical moment in the series: "like Alfred Hitchcock, I have strolled through one of my scenes: as Reinhart is about to board the airplane that will carry him back to the USA, in *Crazy in Berlin*, he is bored by a tall thin T/5 with heavy eyebrows arched in perpetual curiosity. I did indeed at that time weigh about 160 lbs" (11 February 1977).

Perhaps the most intriguing assessment of this relationship between author and character has been offered by Alan Wilde, who sees in Reinhart's experiences a reflection of Berger's life as a novelist, "manifest most obviously, perhaps, in the gradual tempering of the humanism to which both originally subscribe." Wilde's sophisticated attempt to advance a phenomenology of Berger's writing reduces astutely questions of resemblance or parallels between Reinhart and his creator to the crucial concern of both with acts of self-definition.[8]

In part because they do seem in some ways to constitute a sociological epic of a familiar sort, in part because they seem on their surface to reveal autobiographical connections, and in part simply because Reinhart is one of the most compellingly drawn characters in American fiction, this series has received the most intense critical scrutiny of Berger's novels—with the exception of *Little Big Man*. Major articles by Ihab Hassan, Douglas A. Hughes, Richard Schickel, Ronald R. Janssen, Sanford Pinsker, Myron Simon, and Alan Wilde have secured for the Reinhart books the kind of sustained critical attention Berger's writing merits and richly rewards.[9]

On the other hand, most of Berger's comments about the Reinhart series reveal a deeply rooted ambivalence, suggesting that while Reinhart holds no great fascination for his creator, writing the books in which he appears may—at distinct moments in Berger's career. For example, in 1978 Berger noted that he had just tried and failed, for the second time, "to resuscitate" Reinhart for a fourth novel. "I confess he has become rather an old bore, which of course is my difficulty and not his. But the kind of life he encounters no longer interests me. The Reinhart books are in a way an answer to the journalism that was contemporaneous with them. I now no longer read the newspapers" (1 August 1978).

Yet, if Reinhart had grown too familiar, the form of his appearances had not, no two novels in the series displaying quite the same narrator or prose style, also a phenomenon accurately noted by Berger:

A book of mine is impossible to comprehend unless it is approached with a regard to its personality, which is certain to be at least subtly different from each to each. The Reinhart books, for example: to me, they have little resemblance among themselves; sometimes it seems as though three different novelists have dealt with the same character, in three styles and according to three sets of values. That the Reinhart of *Crazy* would eventually turn up as the Reinhart of *Vital Parts* is preposterous, as unlikely in fact as that the Eagle Scout of today would be tomorrow's mass murderer—but of course that transformation happens regularly in America: so you see that behind my mask I actually do have a banal moralistic smirk. (24 Feb 1978)

A later letter further details Berger's sense of the differences among these novels: "As to the styles of the Reinhart books: there are four, one for each novel, and if I write two more there will be six. Each novel has its appropriate style. . . . *Crazy* for example employs a Germanic kind of English, *Reinhart* is one of the few—no, make that the only 'comic novel' I've ever written; though the banal boneheads of the newspaper reviews invariably miscall me a comic (novelist). *Vital Parts* is a socio-political diatribe. *Reinhart's Women* is about nourishment" (16 October 1981).

Indeed, *Reinhart's Women*, published some two years after Berger's comment that he had lost interest in the series, confirmed the staying power of the uniquely varied Reinhart format, as well as of Reinhart's character. Speaking in 1986 with Steve Paul of the *Kansas City Star*, Berger noted the saving aspect of Reinhart's otherwise off-putting (to Berger) contemporaneity: "I've kept up with him. I always know what he's doing at any given time. When I write about Reinhart, it's when I'm looking for something to write about. If I try some other things and don't seem to be getting anywhere, I can always go back to Reinhart, because he's someone I know. He's my buddy."[10] And so, finally—and perhaps paradoxically— must each of the Reinhart novels be seen as close to the center of Berger's creative vision. Both individually and collectively, these novels may represent a personal dialectic, revealing an aesthetic conflict, in a way Berger allows in his writing to no single character or theme. As Berger himself noted while writing *Reinhart's Women:* "It always happens in the Reinhart books that the narrative grows longer than one would think at the outset and I must go back and compensate by cutting the girth. But the suspense builds as day after day the end eludes me, and I cannot sleep by night and have stomach aches by day. I believe this happens only with, or mainly with, the Reinhart books" (13 October 1980).

Crazy in Berlin

Not too much can or should be claimed, even in retrospect, of the first sentence of a first novel, but the opening sentence of *Crazy in Berlin*, now some thirty years past its birth, suggests several important constants in the Reinhart series, as well as the syntactic precision that is ever the goal of Berger's prose: "In the twilight, the bust appeared to be of some cocked-hat Revolutionary War Hero of not the very first rank, that is, not G. Washington but perhaps one of those excellent Europeans noted in fact and apocrypha for throwing their weight on our side, Lafayette, say, or von Steuben" (3). This particular perception, as is true of most of Reinhart's, is controlled by the verb *appeared*, and in Berger's novels appearance and reality seldom coincide. This is particularly true of the Reinhart books, but with the peculiar twist that in these novels appearance usually *appears fake*, revealing patently self-serving, mendacious underpinnings—only to be so recontextualized by fate as to finally emerge as more or less true: the tidy distinction implied above between "fact and apocrypha" usually breaks down in Reinhart's experience—as it does in our reading of his exploits. Reinhart's black friend, Splendor Mainwaring, specifies this principle when he chides, "The truth of life is that things are exactly as they appear, and symbols are the bunk." Of course Splendor himself never appears to Reinhart as other than a symbol, thus infinitely complicating the proposition.

Characteristically qualified with absurd precision (a "Revolutionary War Hero of not the very first rank, . . . one of those excellent Europeans noted in fact and apocrypha"), the initial sentence of *Crazy in Berlin* also reveals Reinhart's irrepressible tendency to digress either upward or downward on the ladder of abstraction, ever spinning the concreteness of his experience into something larger or smaller—a manic predilection for theorizing his life. Concept spinning always engages Reinhart's imagination, and in each novel he leaves behind a wake of propositions—all credible, some persuasive, most self-deprecating—as he negotiates the shallows and depths of his life. That Reinhart, standing in the rubble of postwar Berlin, would describe a statue there in terms of the American revolutionary war reveals the stubborn provincialism of even his remarkably enlightened outlook, while subsequent qualifications reveal his characteristic attempt to work through the limitations of that vision.

It is also characteristic that Reinhart has this perception while urinating on the statue, as it turns out, of Friedrich der Grosse—a discovery that inexorably leads Reinhart to observe that his action "was a gross thing to do . . . because he was just educated enough to recall vaguely old Frederick out at Sans

Souci with Voltaire, writing in French, representing the best, or the worst, of one tradition or the other." As it also turns out, Friedrich will be only the first in a series of "statues," the rest in flesh and blood, that Reinhart will encounter in Berlin; each of these characters also represents the best or the worst (often at once) of "one tradition or the other"—Nazism, nihilism, Judaism, Americanism, communism—as well as the more fundamental concepts of friendship, victimization, and survival.

The relation of *Crazy in Berlin* to the canon of postwar American novels is much like Reinhart's relation to Friedrich's statue: irreverent but mindful of the mythologies. In the first place, almost alone among protagonists in postwar American novels, Reinhart genuinely likes the army, finding in it both security and sensibility, his rationale encapsulated by Berger in one gloriously extended sentence:

A society grounded on common inconvenience, where friendship was innocent of opportunism and tolerance flourished without manifesto: no crime could outlaw youth from this company; no merit beyond the grossest went recognized; where sensitivity was soon reduced to coarseness and ambition stifled; where lethargy was rewarded and disenchantment celebrated; this cul-de-sac off the superhighway to the glorious Houyhnhnm of the future where a chicken would stew in every pot and each man be his own poet, unarmed, owing allegiance to one world—this splendid, dear, degrading society, here as nowhere else Reinhart felt at home and loved. (CIB, 304)

More important, however, Reinhart's German-American heritage leads him to investigate recent history from a perspective quite unlike that explored in the much better codified tradition of Jewish-American fiction. At once fearful of some genetic flaw capable of giving birth to Nazi atrocities and German complacence and resentful of the inexorable appropriation of moral high ground, at terrible cost, by Jewish victims of German nihilism, Reinhart struggles to understand and to individualize the universality of moral chaos.

One sure sign of Reinhart's complicated thought appears in his ability to detest nazism while acknowledging some of its perverse appeal to the individual:

In almost every way but the accepted idea of common decency, he felt himself at odds with the world, a kind of Nazi without swastika, without revolver and gas ovens, without the specific enemies—indeed, it was a crazy feeling, an apparently motiveless identification, for although it did not include the trappings, it did comprehend the evil, as when you awoke from a nightmare of murder and for hours afterward despite the evidence of daylight and routine believed yourself an assassin; and worst of all, coexistent with the guilt, the memory of a terribly depraved yet almost romantic pride: *once, anyway, you were not a victim.* (68)

What particularly haunts him is the realization that nazism was a human rather than a German phenomenon and that he himself is subject to "that passion to destroy simply because it could be got away with, because one had been trained all his life to respect and abide by the constraints and then found in a crisis that they held no water" (67). This determination to get beneath the easy surface rationales of ideology, a constant in Berger's writing, will be echoed in *Nowhere*, when Russell Wren has a similar reaction to terrorism: "Frankly, I think the urge to destroy comes first, and then he who has it looks for a slogan to mouth while blowing up people and things, with the idea that his mayhem thereby becomes perfectly reasonable" (19).

Perceptive enough to sense that in Berlin's devastation "all the crap has been blasted away, leaving something honest," Reinhart must reconcile humanistic commonplaces with the sometimes more complicated propositions of his own experience, among them his intuitive grasp of the necessary reciprocity of victims and victimizers. Derided by a blind Jewish doctor for his liberal belief that "there is wisdom in a wound," Reinhart nevertheless wishes that he himself "had a grievance," since "being without one in the modern world was disabling." But he acknowledges the complicated countervailing principle that "people use us as we ask them to: this is life's fundamental, and often the only, justice" (310). As a result, his view of conflicting ideologies often evolves from questions of right and wrong to more profound questions about the differences between reality and its masks. Harvey Swados praised the uniqueness of this enterprise in a 1958 *New Leader* review. "This is not however the traditional liberal American novel in which the well-intentioned writer sighs over the pity of it all and invites us as readers to sigh with him while he hates the Nazi as his enemy and loves the Jew as his brother. That we can do for ourselves. What Berger has done instead is to commence where liberalism ends, in the world of ideas."[11]

A blond, heavily muscled, twenty-one-year-old U.S. Army medic corporal in Allied-occupied Berlin, Reinhart has cornered the market on guilt. He complains to Nathan Schild, a Jewish intelligence officer: "I'm sick of being made to feel a swine because I'm of German descent. I'm sick of being in the privileged class that nothing ever happens to. I'm tired of being big and healthy, but I can't help it, I was born that way. If you would be a prisoner in any concentration camp ever made, I would be a guard. Now, you know everything—but do you know that? How that makes a person feel? Do you know what it is to be in debt to everybody?" (365). Schild evokes Reinhart's contradictory attitudes toward Jews, as a string of other acquaintances forces him to confront a range of ideologies associated with politics, philosophy, gender, and nationality.

Among the grotesques Reinhart meets are: Bach, a giant invalid who strenuously advances the case for subtle anti-Semitism, arguing that overt persecution has just made the Jew stronger, even as it is revealed that for four years he hid his Jewish wife from the Nazis; Dr. Otto Knebel, a former communist tortured in a Russian concentration camp and now a fascist; Schatzi, an early S.A. activist betrayed by Hitler, imprisoned for four years in Auschwitz as a gentile criminal, and now a cynical Russian agent; Lichenko, a deserter from the Russian army and enthusiastic would-be capitalist given temporary refuge by Schild, who, it should be noted, is himself an idealistic communist and a traitor. Above all else, these characters are survivors, although the diversity of their lives and outlooks can only confound Reinhart's simple humanism. Finally, Reinhart's amour propre requires that he juggle his love and sex lives (the two never quite at one) among three quite different women: a whorish sixteen-year-old German girl; her older, sadder, wiser (and to Reinhart infinitely more desirable) married Jewish cousin; and a robust American nurse.

Although Reinhart gradually emerges from the novel as Berger's narrative focus—much as he leaves Berlin as the sole true survivor among its major characters—point of view in *Crazy in Berlin* is switched among Reinhart, Schild, Schatzi, and Lichenko. The interactions of these characters structure a number of complicated dialectics, both for Reinhart and for Berger's readers. More important, as Gerald Weales has explained, this narrative scheme filters all ideological propositions through multiple possible interpretations. Citing one of Schild's internal conflicts, occasioned by the memory of a friend executed for Trotskyite deviation by Stalinist comrades in the Spanish civil war, Weales isolates the real strength of Berger's method in its allowing the reader to look "through Schild looking through Grossman," which has the effect of presenting "abstract ideas as no more invulnerable to the individual vision than lust or greed."[12]

Beneath the paratactic clashes of ideology that occasion much of the dialogue in *Crazy in Berlin*, Reinhart's enduring quest is for freedom, a definition of self free from the expectations and opprobrium of others. His visual model for this dream is the knight in Durer's etching *Ritter, Tod, und Teufel*, and this picture, obviously important to Berger, will later provide a visual paradigm for some of his description in *Neighbors*. Admiring the knight because he is serving "his time in the gully of death and the devil" and must do so completely alone, Reinhart tells Schild: "If you glance quickly at the picture you won't see anything but the Knight . . . but most of all that wonderful tough face, sure of itself, looking not at the airy castle or horseshit Death or the mangy Devil, because they'll all three get him soon enough, but he doesn't care. He is complete in himself—isn't that what integrity means?—and he is proud of it, because he is smiling a little" (360).

In Ihab Hassan's words, more "clowning knight errant" than knight, Reinhart can never live up to his model, but he comes close when he risks his own life in an unsuccessful attempt to save Schild—who has refused further collaboration—from being abducted by two Communist agents. Reinhart, who has unsuccessfully matched wits and will with opponents throughout the novel, now matches bare-handed strength against a giant assailant and wins, killing him, but not before Schild is murdered by the other attacker or before Reinhart suffers a serious wound, inevitably to his head. The exterior wound heals, but Reinhart's guilt over his true motives for helping Schild, to his thinking actually a form of betrayal, drives him to the psycho ward—where, characteristically, he begins to consider the advantages of becoming a psychiatrist. " Like knighthood, this profession gave you a permanent upper hand; like the priesthood, it made everybody else feel guilty and also grateful; like the Jews it was much reviled yet indispensable and always right" (422). Gradually freeing himself, not from guilt, but from its debilitating effects, Reinhart recovers enough to get shipped home, his recovery certified by a final betrayal, this time perfectly justified, of the cynical Schatzi, who has managed to sneak onto Reinhart's evacuation flight.

Reinhart in Love

The literal situation of *Crazy in Berlin* provides the figurative atmosphere for the next two Reinhart books, as Berger makes of his great protagonist a kind of permanent-occupation soldier of the soul, someone always stationed in foreign territory. Regardless of place or time, and no matter how outrageous the particulars of his situation, Reinhart remains the eternal outsider, denied both the moral satisfaction of the victor and the clear abasement of the vanquished. In love, commerce, and culture, Reinhart always manages to be in the wrong place at the wrong time, his wondering nature a kind of magnet for the impositions of others.

Reinhart is greeted upon his return from the army by an endearingly meek and unassuming father, whose greatest joy seems to come from reciting advertising labels and basking in the glories of postwar commodification, and by a mother (Maw) who hails his arrival by snarling, "Here come six more shirts per week." Reinhart's initial problems lie in coming to terms with his

parents, since he seems more displaced at home than he was in the grotes-
query of Berlin. Dad dispenses great advice for consuming, but none for living, and Reinhart struggles to reconcile his own romantic concerns, indicated
by words such as "*paladin, epic, paramour, gourmet, wastrel, mistress, cognac,
intrepid, leather, bronze, crimson, alabaster, lance, battle-ax*" with the dreary
terms he associates with his Dad: "*commerce, economics, exchange, real prop-
erty, securities, stocks, bonds, finance, annuities, comptrollers, town planning
boards, auditors, accountants, ledgers*" (112). Reinhart senses that "those two
vocabularies are not entirely incompatible," but they represent in his own life
alternating sirens, one vocabulary ever luring him back just as he most desires
to embrace the other.

Maw's hostility toward everything reaches epic proportions and seems calculated to preclude all of Reinhart's interests. Warning her son to avoid
"truck with Filth" or she will slip him strychnine, her definition of *Filth* taking in most aspects of modern life, Maw zeroes in on sex, which will indeed
also prove to be a problem for Reinhart. Her concern: "Why, Smut. All the
dirty, miserable, horrible things that bachelors in boarding houses think
about; what goes on among the niggers in back alleys in the dead of night;
what makes cats do that terrible evil whining in the wee hours and dogs run
in packs with their tongues hanging out so disgusting; what ruined Gladys
Welch. People touching one another in secret ways" (114).

Reinhart in Love moves Reinhart from the rubble of Berlin to the bustle of
postwar American business, from an economy of scarcity—whether of material goods or of spirit—to an economy of excess, from the nightmares of the
German past to the absurdities of the American dream. Discharged from the
army, in which he had been happy, Reinhart returns to civilian life, which he
finds singularly disastrous. His comic misadventures are guided by Claude
Humbold, a wonderfully opportunistic real estate agent and con man for
whom Reinhart reluctantly works, by the enterprising and calculating
Genevieve Raven, whom he is tricked into marrying, and by Splendor Mainwaring, his talented but erratic black friend, who has a special talent for getting Reinhart into impossible situations. "He was still twenty-one and had
never had another profession; he feared America, people, and life—not really
but poetically, which was worse" (4). Reinhart's fears are real, his anguish serious, but his experiences in this novel are clearly comic, and *Reinhart in Love*
is the only one of his books Berger terms a comedy.

While this second Reinhart book chronicles its protagonist's hapless
courtship and marriage, its title applies more broadly to the debilitating fact
that "*Reinhart was in love with everything*" (112). In a drunken moment he
grandly declares that his purpose is "not to bury life, but to recognize it," and

he instructs that this may be accomplished if one is careful to "do no harm and always uphold the dignity of human life" (133). Unfortunately, the arrangement rarely seems reciprocal. People, ideas, culture, even banality intoxicate Reinhart with an openness to experience that soon proves ruinous: civilian life buries him just as surely as do the medical commodities that tumble from his father's fantastically stuffed medicine chest. Awed in Berlin by historic rubble, Reinhart is stunned at home by the excess of commodities and the pervasiveness of economic hype. The most exuberantly written of the Reinhart books, this is Berger's one true comic novel, a wonderful compendium of funny scenes and hilarious rhetoric.

The grotesque philosopher-teachers, all gravely crippled in some respect, who so largely determined Reinhart's experience in Berlin have been supplanted in this novel by a gloriously crooked realtor, Claude Humbold, who instructs Reinhart in the wonders of business. "This is bidness," Claude impatiently explains, "not them silly games like plugging Fachists, or Commonists, whatever them Heinies was at the time" (151). As well versed in the rhetoric of success as in the practice of chicanery, Claude gives Reinhart advice strikingly at odds with the old world cynicism of his former Berlin mentors. "Always keep a positive face towards life, bud. When you're losing money, up your buying. If you get beat up once, start a fight with a bigger fella. That's the way of Jesus Christ, bud, who got out and walked on the water when his boat leaked. Nothing stopped that tough little guy, because his sainted mother was behind him all the way" (156).

What distinguishes Claude in Reinhart's experience is that he is both a survivor and a success, even when things don't seem to be going his way. Bolstered by an outrageously self-serving philosophy that casts God as "the greatest bidnessman of them all," Claude can explain away any setback and defend any action, and he ultimately involves Reinhart in a patently fraudulent scheme hatched by Claude and crooked politicians to get a city contract for sewers that will never be built.

Reinhart and Splendor end up as officers of the phony sewer construction company, affording Reinhart an oblique opportunity to consider what it means to be an American Negro in somewhat the same way that in *Crazy in Berlin* he considered what it means to be a Jew. Finally realizing that in his unpredictable expansiveness and frequent personal disasters—resulting from a persistent refusal to do as expected—Splendor has become another teacher, Reinhart sees in Splendor's freedom from limitations a new gauge of his own failure. "My friend," Reinhart wryly concludes, "you have out-Reinharted Reinhart—you are all I ever wanted to be, and twice as vivid" (392). When Reinhart and Splendor decide to force the actual construction of the sewer, an

amok power shovel destroys much of the black neighborhood they were attempting to serve. This seeming disaster, however, perfectly serves the interests of yet another of Claude's crooked schemes, and Reinhart's momentary
moral bravery ironically plunges him more deeply into Claude's enthusiastic
chicanery.

Vital Parts

"Timing is your trouble, Carl," specifies one of Reinhart's old classmates,
now as obviously a success in life as the now forty-four-year-old Reinhart is a
failure. The acquaintance, Bob Sweet, an updated and hip version of Claude
Humbold, is right, of course, but the strong evidence of the first three
Reinhart books suggests that as much could be said of time itself—that
Reinhart's struggle is always with time as well as, or more than, just timing.
"Reinhart is, in a very real sense," Berger has ventured, "always up to the min-
ute (whether or not the world is): indeed, trying to be so seems his difficulty"
(17 May 1977).

Its narrative strongly bound to the specific time of 1945, *Crazy in Berlin*
surveyed a momentous historical period as it filtered through Reinhart's consciousness. Set only a year later, *Reinhart in Love* concerned itself less with the
historical moment of postwar America than with the crucial private time of
Reinhart's life as he struggled through his initiation into marriage and commerce. *Vital Parts* intensifies and combines both kinds of temporal focus—
public and private—as it explores Reinhart's middle-aged reactions to the
cultural turmoil of the late sixties. Here Reinhart's problems with his fashionably rebellious son, Blaine, and Reinhart's affair with a young girl focus
the background concerns of the years in which time itself seemed the crux of
cultural turmoil—the late sixties. Moreover, Reinhart, clearly time's victim,
finds himself involved in yet another wild scheme, one to cheat death
through cryonics. For Reinhart, one of the great appeals of a plan for freezing
the dead for possible reanimation in the future is that it would "eliminate the
dimension of Time, by which most social situations are measured" (124).

Measured by time, the Reinhart of *Vital Parts* has hit bottom. His body an
overweight wreck, his marriage a disaster, his various commercial enterprises all
failed, hated by a surly son and adored by a helplessly naive daughter, Reinhart
derives his only satisfaction now from self-pity. "You are only beaten if you
think so," exhorts Reinhart to himself, only to reach the appalling conclusion
"But I think so." Ticking off his diminished prospects, this eternal optimist
now manages a bleak inventory. "I am just a guy who regardless of what he
thought at twenty knows at forty-four only that he will die" (43). Resentment,

long an adversary Reinhart managed to keep under control, now seems his primary emotion as he complains:

> Somehow I have always missed the advantage, and this has probably warped me with jealousy. Ever since I was born I have had to listen incessantly to someone else's propaganda, and not only an account of their superiorities, but, what is worse, their pains, for which they have always contrived to make me responsible. As a youth I was a pleasure-loving punk, as an adult I am a bully, as a white man a former slaveholder, as a member of the middle class an all- purpose exploiter. When in good shape I was thought to be stupid and insensitive, and now as overweight and with short breath, I am considered ugly and moribund. (79)

Of course, one reason Reinhart does always seem to miss the advantage is his one-directional philosophical bent, which can rationalize any outrage, imposition, or unfairness of which he is the victim, while forgiving no embarrassment or blunder that he commits. For example, confronted by hi˙ sneering, slogan-spouting son, emblem of all Reinhart abhors in his society, he calmly realizes:

> Blaine played a ruthless game. He was a pacifist when asked to go to war, an advocate of violent demonstrations for Negroes and college students, a believer in free love for anyone under thirty and repression for those older: he had contempt for money and those who earned it but demanded to be given as much as he needed; he dressed and comported himself flagrantly so as to attract attention, yet getting it he derided and/or denounced his audience.
> He was, in short, altogether human and absolutely normal. There was no mistaking his commitment to injustice, to incessant provocation, to maximum publicity, illogic, malice, attachment to his own crowd and frightened hatred of any other, his solipsism, his nightmares, his sadism, or his relationship to his father. You wouldn't find him tormenting a stranger. He loved his old dad. (62)

Although he senses the ironies and injustices in an age when "a man could be termed a crypto-Nazi merely for shaving off his sideburns, a genocide because he deplores a mob, and a bully for questioning the credentials of folksinger-statesmen," Reinhart no longer has the spirit to resist. In his disparagement of the age, Reinhart undoubtedly does reflect some of his creator's dissatisfaction. Berger told Douglas Hughes that he did indeed hate "the disruption of the 1960s," believing them to be "as threatening to individual freedom as what they attacked." Berger specified, "My objection to the so-called counterculture was precisely the same as that I should make against the culture itself: that it is tyrannically sentimental, intellectually vulgar, and morally infantile."[13]

Assaulted by the superficial rhetoric of TV hip talk, the psycho-babble of an obviously twisted pop psychiatrist, and by the patent contradictions of his son's revolutionary sloganeering, Reinhart sadly concludes that his is "no civilization in which to live the life of the mind," even as all other lives seem closed to him. "Human beings are vile," is his best advice to a young girl with whom he has an unsatisfying affair, qualifying this dark philosophy only with the specification that "like any other general rule it has as many exceptions as applications" (179).

But Reinhart in despair is still Reinhart. After volunteering to be the first living human to be frozen for Sweet's cryonics foundation, and deciding to spend his last days using foundation money to buy into fantasies of success and power, he begins to feel the relief of "gradually jettisoning the ballast of moral judgment." Just as surely as he believes people are vile, he also realizes they are all that interest him, concluding, "Vile they might well be, but it happens that vileness is fascinating—to a degree, of course." And when Winona, his fat, hopelessly innocent daughter, reveals to him just how much she needs his protection, he determines to live and to have her live with him.

Reinhart's Women

In *Reinhart's Women* the now fifty-four-year-old Reinhart finally discovers something he can do well: cooking. The novel finds Reinhart ten years after his divorce from Genevieve, living with and supported by his daughter, Winona, now a beautiful and successful fashion model. His son, Blaine, last seen as a surly radical in *Vital Parts*, now is a surly, snobbish, and successful stockbroker, unchanged in his disdain for his father. Having finally admitted that he is hopeless as a businessman, Reinhart has withdrawn from the world and contents himself with managing his daughter's household and with cooking "in a spirit of scientific inquiry."

Actually, cooking has become for him both an aesthetic and a philosophy, and for the first time in his life "he did not feel as if he were either charlatan or buffoon." "Food," Reinhart notes, "is really kinder than people" (57). The sense of freedom so long denied him now seems in reach as Reinhart defines himself—even as a cook—in his own terms. Ever generous, he tries to share this discovery with his mean-spirited son, now hobbled by self-image worries much like those that plagued the Reinhart of old: "But the funny thing is that, without benefit of a movement, I am liberated from all sorts of restraints, including those I have imposed on myself. It was ridiculous that I lived almost half a century trying to measure up to the principles of other people" (46).

Still an inveterate concept-spinner, Reinhart has finally seen that he "does better by looking at the eggs in hand rather than at the souffle to come." Now, however, his propositions seem more modest and more profound, perhaps shaped from the residues of his longstanding skirmishes with unsatisfactory moral codes. A newfound ability to suspend judgment now characterizes his manner, since he has learned "that a good many claims in life are never put to the test, and from those that are, often enough, truth still does not issue, and finally in the rare event that it does, even rarer is to find the mortal to whom it matters" (223).

Confronted with plans for a suspiciously idealistic commune led by the ex-black-militant son of his old friend Splendor Mainwaring and financed in part by his own venal son Blaine, Reinhart makes no real effort to decide whether the project is fraudulent or sincere, reflecting instead that "most enterprises since the Renaissance have necessarily partaken of both the honest and the bogus in equal amounts to preserve the balance known as modern civilization" (53).

Even more global is his advice to his daughter, Winona, advice starkly contrasting with his bitter "humans are vile" sentiments offered another young girl in *Vital Parts*. Now Reinhart focuses on the processes of life rather than judging the outcomes of those processes: "Every living thing already knows everything it needs to know: how to succeed, how to fail, how to survive, and how to perish. Sometimes we pretend we don't know, but we know all right. The older I get, the more I realize that nothing is a genuine surprise" (62).

Reinhart's new, quiet confidence stems from his finding in cooking the concrete metaphor around which to organize his philosophy. Calmly acknowledging that "the human animal, from pup to patriarch, was such a bizarre creature" and that "human relations remained a good deal less explicable than anything in atomic physics," Reinhart has forged his profound equanimity from one certain starting point: "of all the activities of human beings, there is one thing that they alone, in all the world, do, and that is: cook the food they eat" (261). Praised for this observation by a TV executive who bubbles, "Carlo, you're a philosopher," Reinhart replies, "Naw. . . . I'm better than that! I'm a cook" (262).

What Reinhart has discovered is that metaphors of nourishment, a concept indispensable for the spirit, have a physical origin, profound in its own right:

Food was a great positive, yea-saying force, the ultimate source of vitality—until a phase of the cycle was completed and oneself became food for the worms. It is only through food that we survive, and we die when we are fed on too heartily by microbes, or by the crab named cancer who eats us alive. In the emotional realm there is no more eloquent metaphor: lovers feed on one another, and passion is devouring. A philosopher lives on food for thought. One is what one eats, and eats what one is. (70)

This most extended of the string of propositions spun out throughout the Reinhart series reveals that Reinhart has finally found a spot in his universe where language and concrete reality are not at odds.

Long completely at the mercy of unmerciful women, particularly his mother and his ex-wife, Reinhart can now even take in stride the news that his daughter is having a lesbian affair with a successful older businesswoman. Age has taught him that "the best defense against any moral outrage is patience: wait a moment and something will change: the outrage, he who committed it, or, most often, oneself." So long victimized by being out of step with his time, Reinhart has finally achieved the kind of understanding that is timeless.

Winona's lover (a female version of the con men who have always directed Reinhart's forays into business) contrives to lure him back into the world, first as a supermarket-product demonstrator, then as a guest "chef" for a spot appearance on a local TV show, and the novel closes with the strong prospect of Reinhart's having his own show, "Chef Carlo Cooks." His apparent successes, however, are not confined to the kitchen, as Reinhart escapes the gentle and loving tyranny of his daughter, emerges unscathed from an encounter with his ex-wife, and begins a promising relationship with a young woman who seems in many ways a female version of himself—intelligent, considerate, awkward. In fact, Reinhart begins to gather around him a small band of kindred souls, hoping to buy and run a quaint small-town café. Once again the lure of business proves irresistible for Reinhart, and once again the prospect of disaster cannot be discounted, but this time the odds seem more in Reinhart's favor. Jonathan Baumbach has summed up this most recent of the Reinhart books as "Berger's most graceful and modest book, a paean to kindness and artistry, a work of quiet dazzle."[14]

And another account of Reinhart's odyssey seems a good bet. When asked following the publication of *Reinhart's Women* whether Reinhart might appear again, Berger replied, "I won't know what becomes of him until he tells me, but I suspect that he'll be heard from again, probably when he could be said to be authentically an old man."[15]

Reinhart may be Berger's greatest creation, and the Reinhart series to date spans Berger's career, a monument at once to its manic diversity and to its underlying unity. Both the vitality and the vision of the Reinhart books offer ample evidence that Berger is one of America's most original and most gifted novelists: in Reinhart's singularity, Berger most effectively lets us find ourselves.

Chapter Three

The Myths of the Old West: *Little Big Man*

In a very profound sense, all of Berger's novels can be thought of as captivity narratives, his characters all incarcerated in the prison house of language. Yet two of Berger's most celebrated novels, *Little Big Man* and *Arthur Rex*, are captivity narratives in a much more literal sense, the former written in the well-codified frontier description of life in the captivity of Indians, the latter reflecting, as does its primary source, the fact that the great telling of the Arthurian legend was by a prisoner, Sir Thomas Malory. *Little Big Man* is Berger's response to the great American myth of the frontier, representing as it does most of the central traditions of American literature. With *Arthur Rex*, Berger takes on Arthurian legend, the Matter of Britain, one of the great traditions in British literary history and no less a vital national myth. Together, these two novels best represent the range of Berger's style, the depth of his commitment to great literary traditions, and the complexity of his vision. If the Reinhart novels are perhaps Berger's greatest achievement, these two are certainly his most carefully researched, most historically resonant, and most thoroughly textured. Accordingly, this and the following chapter will focus exclusively on these two most remarkable and remarkably similar novels, starting with *Little Big Man*, surely Berger's best-known work.

The Achievement of *Little Big Man*

"You must understand that I did not write *Little Big Man* as an exercise in social criticism," Thomas Berger said in an interview. "It was not intended as an indictment of the white man. I wrote it for the same motive that informs all my fiction: to amuse myself."[1] Had Berger never written anything other than *Little Big Man*, he would have earned a respected place in American literary history. Just as surely as there can be no single Great American Novel, *Little Big Man* has by now been almost universally recognized as *a* great American novel, and while its genius was not immediately apparent to large numbers of readers or to all initial reviewers, that genius has been at least implicitly acknowledged by some two dozen scholarly studies and by uninterrupted popular sales in the twenty-five years since it was first published. As L. L. Lee so accurately observed in one of the first articles to give careful consideration to *Little Big Man*: "This is a most American novel. Not just in its subject, its setting, its story (these are common matters), but in its thematic structures, in its dialectic: savagery and civilization, indeed, but also the virgin land and the city, nature and the machine, individualism and community, democracy and hierarchy, innocence and knowledge, all the divisive and unifying themes of the American experience, or, more precisely, of the American 'myth.'"[2]

Surely Frederick Turner was correct when he concluded in his 1977 reassessment of *Little Big Man* for the *Nation* that "few creative works of post–Civil War America have had as much of the fiber and blood of the national experience in them."[3] Just as certainly, it is now safe to say that *Little Big Man*, the novel, will more than match its survival skills against those of Jack Crabb, its 111-year-old protagonist. And in some ways *Little Big Man* must be acknowledged as Berger's greatest novel—not necessarily his best, but the one in which he took on the sweeping matter of his American literary and mythological heritage and made a lasting contribution to both.

For all of its genius, however, this novel has proved itself a particular thorn in the side of Berger scholarship: in the challenging canon of a novelist who never repeats himself, *Little Big Man* seems at once the most accessible and the most singular of Berger's novels. Its historical subject matter invites us to check Crabb's narrative for accuracy, and its anthropological introduction to Cheyenne culture invites us to check for both accuracy and understanding. By invoking the figure of Gen. George Armstrong Custer and offering a version of America's most fascinating military defeat, Berger's novel risks assimilation into the cottage industry of "last stand" literature. By developing Jack Crabb's wondering vision and wonderfully witty vernacular voice, the novel almost demands comparison with *Huckleberry Finn*. And because the fictional character of Crabb shares so many aspects with the traditional picaro, notwithstanding the fact that it also shares those aspects with many a "real" character in the Old West, Berger's novel has been seized by critics as an example of a literary tradition older and broader than any American literature could produce for itself.

What must not be overlooked is that each of these inviting (and frequently rewarding) approaches to Berger's third novel attempts to look into the novel by looking at some *other* class of literature and that none of these approaches attempts to consider *Little Big Man* as a Thomas Berger novel, one sharing the vision and style of his other books. Noting this tendency, Berger once suggested that "the best readers of *Little Big Man* are persons who have no interest in the frontier, like the wife of my New York dentist, urban and Jewish" (11 February 1977). Accordingly, while I will examine as many aspects of *Little Big Man* as I can, I will do so more for what this novel can tell us about Berger's style as a novelist than for what it can tell us about the West, the literature of the West, the Cheyenne, Custer, etc.

If, as I believe, the central aspect of Berger's style as a novelist is a thoroughgoing tendency toward dialectic and paratactic structures (by *paratactic*, I mean that seemingly incongruous material has been juxtaposed; parataxis is the *syntax* of putting things together without trying to relate them), this novel may best indicate the multiple levels of meaning on which those structures can operate. For, just as the action of the novel establishes a cultural dialectic between the competing claims of white and Indian society, the style of the novel establishes a more subtle, but ultimately more significant, dialectic between Jack Crabb's story as a model of human consciousness and the manner of that story as a model of literary self-consciousness. In this sense, Jack's existence as a literary construct is even more remarkable than his claim to be the sole white survivor of Custer's last stand.

A Story about Story Telling

Little Big Man is a story purporting to tell the truth about the old American West. It is ostensibly transcribed from the tape-recorded reminiscences of "the late Jack Crabb—frontiersman, Indian scout, gunfighter, buffalo hunter, adopted Cheyenne—in his final days upon this earth." That Jack's final days come some 111 years after his first, and that he claims to have been the sole white survivor of the Battle of the Little Bighorn, put this "truth" in some doubt. Equally strong and contradictory evidence exists that the last of the oldtimers is hopelessly senile and that he is a conscious craftsman of fiction as concerned with developing his own story *as a narrative to be read* as he is with relating the incidents of his life. Furthermore, Jack's narrative comes to us through the patently unreliable editorship of one Ralph Fielding Snell, a fatuously gullible and weak-minded self-professed "man of letters," who not so incidentally reveals a number of parallels between his life and that of his narrator—just as John Ray, Jr., suggests more than incidental overlap with Humbert Humbert in *Lolita*. Snell, who does admit to some doubts about Crabb's story, concedes that he passes on its claims only after his own emotional collapse of some ten years and his foreword and epilogue contain numerous hints that this emotional condition persists. Yet against all of this postmodern self-reflexivity stands the disarming realism of Jack's tale, the authority and credibility of his voice. The action in *Little Big Man* is episodic, its story a macaronic of historical events and personages, its atmosphere the swirling myths that transformed people and events into America's defining epoch: the West. What unites the disparate threads of the novel's action and its swings between the antithetical world views of white and Indian culture is the voice and vision of Jack Crabb, surely one of Berger's greatest achievements. That voice is itself an index to the structure of the book—to its blending of conflicting styles and sources into a stunning synthesis.

Jack's description of his Cheyenne upbringing illustrates his unique ability to combine a child's uncritical (or, on occasion, cynical) acceptance with the cultural insights of an anthropologist:

It ain't bad to be a boy among the Cheyenne. You never get whipped for doing wrong, but rather told: "That is not the way of the Human Beings." One time Coyote started to laugh while he was lighting his father's pipe, because a horsefly was crawling on his belly. This was a serious failure of manners on his part, comparable to a white boy's farting loud in church. His Pa laid away the pipe and said: "On account of your lack of self-control I can't smoke all day without disgusting certain Persons in the other world. I wonder if you aren't a Pawnee instead of a Human Being." Coyote went out upon the prairie and stayed there alone all night to hide his shame.

You have got to *do things right* when you're a Cheyenne. (67)

Whatever else may be said of Jack, let there be no doubt that *he gets things right* whenever he speaks of Indian ways. Indeed, Jack's description of Cheyenne life draws heavily from anthropological studies such as E. Adamson Hoebel's *Cheyennes: Indians of the Great Plains* (1960) and George Bird Grinnell's *Fighting Cheyennes* (1956). In the guise of simply describing his life with the Cheyenne, Jack manages to explain or imply almost every one of the sixteen postulates and nineteen corollaries identified by Hoebel as forming "the bedrock upon which the Cheyennes have raised their cultural edifice, which is for them The Cheyenne Way."[4] In like fashion, almost all of Jack's major experiences with the Cheyenne derive from historical or anthropological fact. Chapter 4, "Pronghorn Slaughter," for example, very closely follows Hoebel's description of the mystic procedure of the antelope surround,[5] and Old Lodge Skins's story of the bravery of Little Man closely follows Grinnell's account of the death of Mouse's Road.[6] Jack's first return to white society takes place when Cheyenne magic against bullets proves powerless against a cavalry saber charge, an incident drawn directly from the Battle of Solomon's Fork on 29 July 1857, noted by Grinnell as "perhaps the only occasion on which a large body of troops charged Indians with the

saber."[7] When Jack returns to Old Lodge Skins's band, his reappearance conflicts with the myth the Cheyenne have developed to explain his loss at
Solomon's Fork. "It is true . . . that there is a thing here that I do not understand," admits one of his Indian captors, almost certainly echoing a remark
by Plenty-Coups to Frank Linderman: "There is Something here! Something
that does not wish you to understand."[8]

Likewise, when Jack speaks of Custer or the cavalry, the fine points and
drawbacks of specific handguns, the growth of frontier cities, or other matters of white culture, he is equally accurate and often equally insightful. Leave
it to Jack not only to detail the logistics and tactics of buffalo hunting but also
to suggest that the decimation of the buffalo should not be dismissed as a
primitivist tragedy or a crime against nature. Jack dutifully reminds his readers that Indians "was frequently hungry long before the buffalo had been
eliminated, and even more so before the white man made his appearance,
prior to which they never had the horse from which to hunt, nor the gun with
which to shoot a buffalo at long range while afoot" (336).

Jack's experiences and impressions are woven from a mad mélange of histories, memoirs, biographies, legends, novels, and even movies about the
West; and it is a mark of Berger's pervasive irony that most of these sources
are put by him to uses antithetical to the intent or bias of the original authors.
For example, Jack's impression of Old Lodge Skins's camp ("I see their
dump, but where's the town?") may owe much to scenes such as that of the
Ogillallah village recorded by Francis Parkman in *The Oregon Trail*, as may
Jack's low opinion of Indian dogs.[9] Jack's Cheyenne foil and nemesis,
Younger Bear, may be partially modeled after a vain Indian described by
Parkman, and the browbeating of Younger Bear by his wife has much in
common with another scene in Parkman's narrative. Yet, while Parkman may
have helped inspire the events and images of Berger's novels, Jack's narrative
stands as an evenhanded corrective to Parkman's sentimental excesses and
cultural biases. As is true in the case of most of the sources Berger drew from,
Jack's narrative does not echo Parkman's, but engages it as another level in
the comprehensive dialectic of Berger's structure.

There is simply no way of knowing how many of Jack's experiences, in
matters both small and large, Berger directly or indirectly drew from other
sources. In acknowledging and specifying many of those sources, Berger has
said of his research, "After reading some seventy books about the Old West I
went into a creative trance in which it seemed as though I were listening to
Jack Crabb's narrative" (18 December 1984). The artistry of *Little Big
Man*, however, has much more to do with Berger's principles of selection,
combination, and comment than with facticity. As anyone intent on working

with Berger's sources soon realizes, the facts of Indian life do not constitute art, and while rereading the balance of the sources Berger has identified is more than enough to put anyone in a trance, that trance is by no means guaranteed to be creative. As folklorist Frederick Turner has explained, the vast majority of the enormous body of literature dealing with Plains Indians and the Plains Indian campaigns is derivative or polemical "crap that the general public has done well to let alone." Berger's genius, says Turner, lay in using this body of material to bring to life a cultural dialogue between whites and Indians in which, "for the first time really in American letters, *both* cultures are seen from the inside out."[10]

Although the accuracy of Jack's details has been noted by several critics, most notably Leo E. Oliva, what has been overlooked is that Jack also offers a folksy-sounding but astute critical commentary on the literature of the West, including such helpful and accurate rules of thumb for evaluating shootouts as: "When you run into a story of more than three against one and one winning, then you have heard a lie" (293).[11] Indeed, one of the wonderful ironies inherent in Berger's structure of *Little Big Man* is that Jack, the ostensible man of action, reveals much more metaliterary knowledge than does Snell, the ostensible man of letters. Just as surely as Jack's account of his life explores the nature and importance of western myths—both white and Indian—it also explores the linguistic and literary mechanics of myth-making, whether in history, anthropology, journalism, or the novel itself.

Jack Crabb's Critical Voice

In a most subtle fashion, Berger has so crafted Jack's voice as to make it at once a part of, and a comment on, the process through which the Old West has been created by language. On one level, Jack's manipulations of language serve to characterize him as a self-styled teller of tall tales in the best tradition of both white and Indian cultures. On another level, by frequently highlighting precisely his role as fabulator and by repeatedly shifting his focus from events to the ways in which they are approximated and distorted by language, Jack becomes a much sneakier addition to the line of post-modern characters whose self-reflexive aspects argue that the concept of language as subservient to external reality is the central myth of human existence. First and foremost, Jack is a storyteller, with his primary allegiance to language rather than history.

Actually, as Berger would no doubt specify, what we call history *is* language, and perhaps nowhere is this truer than in the case of the "history" of the American frontier. One of the singularly most appropriate ways in which

Berger designed *Little Big Man* as the "Western to end all Westerns" was to make Jack's voice and character such an obvious pastiche of fact and fantasy, of literary myths and received truths. From Cooper onward, the literature of the frontier has been filled with seemingly crude and unlettered characters who ultimately drop their rough personas to reveal either noble birth or genteel background and education (a continuation of the "mysterious stranger" tradition that Fielding devised for *Tom Jones*). Berger plays against this specific convention in Western literature by keeping Jack's persona scrupulously democratic and unprivileged, while allowing just enough narrative sophistication to show through to call Jack's true nature into question. Even more significant in Jack's literary ancestry is the long tradition of so mythologizing frontier and western personages as to make virtually impossible the separation of man from myth.

Henry Nash Smith's *Virgin Land* chronicles this phenomenon from the time of Daniel Boone (some of whose experiences were woven by Cooper into the life of Natty Bumppo) to manufactured heroes such as Kit Carson and Buffalo Bill. William Cody, notes Smith, was practically transformed into the persona of Buffalo Bill by the power of dime novelist Ned Buntline's fictions.[12]

Against such a background in which the literature of the West in many ways managed to become operating reality, the character of Jack Crabb assumes a wonderfully ironic realism in its own right: the more impossible or implausible Berger makes Jack, the more he has in common with the legendary personages of western "history."

Jack himself comments on this phenomenon as it affected Wild Bill Hickok and also as it operated in the Cheyenne mythologizing of Little Big Man. Called out by Hickok, Jack notes that the gunfighter "referred to himself like he was an institution: personally, he didn't care so much about these supposed outrages of mine, but he could not let the noble firm of Wild Bill Hickok, Inc., be loosely dealt with" (320). Showing a remarkable resemblance to white practice in at least this one respect, the Cheyenne so convince themselves that Jack fought bravely then turned into a swallow at the rout at Solomon's Fork that they almost kill him because his existence does not seem to square with their myth. Again Jack astutely notes the mechanics of mythmaking: "If you'll look again at the myth they had built around Little Big Man, you'll see what I mean. It hadn't aught to do with me personally, and insofar as I was to be identified with it, I had to live up to it rather than vice versa. If I did something that would not jibe with the legend, that meant I was not Little Big Man. By this means Indians kept their concepts straight and their heroes untarnished, and did not have to lie" (184–185).

Yet Jack never sounds too objective or too analytical or too self-referential to maintain his persona. Never does his insight obscure his own blindnesses, never do his observations and opinions become completely trustworthy. For instance, his final comment on the Indian mode of mythmaking is "I guess it wouldn't work, though, for somebody who understood the principle of such things as money and the wheel," this notwithstanding his repeated encounters with white legends, such as Hickok and Custer, who are kept "untarnished" in exactly the same manner. Just as his observations about Indian life are consistently understanding, his inherent bias in favor of white culture—a curious blend of stark pragmatism and unbridled idealism—forces him always to shift his attention from the attractive abstract features of the Cheyenne ethos to the concrete deficiencies of its effects, as when he points out that Indians could not invent the wheel even when familiar with its basic mechanics. "You can see that as either invincible ignorance or stubbornness," concludes Jack, "whichever, it's just barbarous" (64).

Rather than actually possessing the wondering vision of a child, Jack merely employs it as a convenient narrative technique, always reserving and usually exercising the right to respond to what he relates. Characteristic enough of his general dilemma, Jack is too accepting to succeed in white society, but not accepting enough to be really comfortable with Indian life. The deeper acceptance shown by Old Lodge Skins, the acceptance at the heart of Cheyenne philosophy, always remains just beyond Jack's grasp. And while he effectively conveys to his audience the idealistic appeal of that philosophy, he also scrupulously chronicles its drawbacks, the greatest of which is simply that it cannot prevail against the white man. The best Jack can achieve is a kind of fragmentary rationalization that victory is not necessarily the true test of a worldview. Having heard Old Lodge Skins tell of the massacre at Sand Creek, noting that the Cheyenne killed there are now on the Other Side, "where there are no white men," Jack draws a distinction between losing and not winning:

The latter designation he pronounced nowadays in a special way: not exactly hateful, for Old Lodge Skins was too much a man to sit about and revile his enemies. That was for a loser, like the Rebs what lost the Civil War. And he wasn't a loser. He wasn't a winner, maybe, but neither was he a failure. You couldn't call the Cheyenne flops unless they had had a railroad engine of their own which never worked as well as the U. P.'s or had invented a gun that didn't shoot straight. (227)

What is perhaps most interesting in Jack's voice, however, is not its cultural relativism but its ability to transcend cultural issues in pursuit of larger truths. While any number of critics have noted Jack's insight into the workings of the specialized epistemologies of Indians, white settlers, gunfighters, and cavalrymen, his ability to synthesize the vagaries of his experience into larger propositions about reality has not been remarked. This ability does not make Jack wise, as the pattern of his personal disasters starkly attests, but it does align him with Berger's other protagonists, all of whom pursue the grail of understanding, usually at considerable personal cost. Reflecting on the ironies of frontier conflict, in which missions of apology and revenge were always uncoordinated and matters of life and death often turned on complicated misunderstandings, Jack sighs that "it would have been ridiculous except it was mortal."

Jack also routinely plays devil's advocate to some of the most dearly held received truths of western lore, as when he examines one of the standard assumptions of popular primitivism: that Indians lived closer to nature than did whites. Citing the permanence of white buildings that established a more concrete and lasting relation to the earth than nomadic Indians could claim, Jack advances the radical proposition that "maybe white men was more natural than Indians."

Finally, he is able to cast even the most famous battle in the history of the Old West into unexpectedly radical terms, seeing it for its unity rather than its conflict: "Looking at the great universal circle, my dizziness grew still. I wasn't wobbling no more. I was there, in movement, yet at the center of the world, where all is self-explanatory merely because it *is*. Being at the Greasy Grass or not, and on whichever side, and having survived or perished, never made no difference. We had all been men. Up there, on the mountain, there was no separations" (443).

Frederick Turner, who has astutely characterized both the genius and the difficulty of *Little Big Man* as arising from Berger's presentation in Jack of a "position beyond sentimentality, beyond classic American liberalism," also notes the way in which Jack finally transcends some of the limitations of both white and Indian worldviews: "He comes to understand both myth and history as radically human constructs. Or, in the novel's terms, he understands what the Cheyenne mean when they say, "This is the way things are," just as he understands the determination of Custer and the whites to make things different. This is a vision sufficiently transcultural to allow Crabb to lament the brutal destruction of the tribal cultures but to see at the same time that even this is, alas, finally human—and thus perhaps inevitable."[13]

Particularly against the backdrop of Jack's occasionally profound and almost always understanding insights into the lives of others, it seems odd that a number of critics have likened his voice to that of Huck Finn, but such a comparison, apart from acknowledging the charm and vitality of

Jack's narration, misleads more than it describes. In the first place, the framing device of Snell's editorship introduces us to Jack precisely in the tradition of southwestern humor from which Twain himself drew so heavily. The relationship between a cultured editor and a backwoods narrator has been termed by Walter Blair "probably the best humorous narrative method employed in the Southwest," and it accentuated the tales of such famous southwestern literary characters as Ovid Bolus, Esq., and Sut Lovingood.[14] Indeed, Jack in many ways parallels Johnson Jones Hooper's Simon Suggs, whose well-known credo was "It is good to be shifty in a new country." (Jack prides himself that even as a boy of ten he was shifty.) The archetypal frontier picaro, Simon Suggs relies on his wits and practices the "ethics of success." Blair describes Suggs as he "moves around the frontier, cheating his father at cards, collecting money on false pretenses from an over-anxious claim-filer, passing himself off as a rich uncle in Augusta, cozening the godly folk at a camp meeting by simulating repentance."[15] Jack is encumbered by far more scruples than is Suggs, but certainly has more in common with him than with the naive and innocent Huck Finn. Unlike Huck, Jack's wondering vision is mostly a pose, one frequently belied by his shrewd analysis of motives and meanings in the situations of his life. While we at times understand more about Jack than he is able to realize himself, our knowledge of those he encounters is limited to, but rarely narrowed by, his insights. Where his own interests are at stake, Jack's reading of human nature invariably defers to wishful thinking, as in his dealings with his business partners or in his adoration of Mrs. Pendrake. When Jack has no immediate stake in the matter, however, his judgment of others can be astonishingly perceptive, as when he explains Custer's depression on the eve of his final battle as arising from the realization that he was too old to remain "the Boy General." Jack observes, "We all know the type of man who hasn't no middle life; from a boyhood continued too long, he falls directly into old age, and it is pathetic" (381).

What is significant here is that Jack routinely advances opinions, explanations, and insights infinitely more complex than those Huck Finn could ever dream of. Partly one of the consequences of Jack's relating boyhood experience from the vantage point of extreme old age, the sophistication of his vision actually seems a solution to the problem Huck's voice posits for American writers who wish to exploit the colloquial style. Richard Bridgman has detailed that problem in his *Colloquial Style in America*, a work whose analysis of Huck's voice makes immediately clear the originality of Jack's. The "central dilemma of the vernacular," specifies Bridgman, is for the writer to figure out "how to escape the limitations a narrator imposes of age, education, regional dialect, topical slang, and occupational jargon, and still preserve something common to all—the essence of the vernacular."[16]

One of Berger's most significant stylistic accomplishments in *Little Big Man* is the creation of just such a voice, as Jack's narrative dramatically captures the essence of the vernacular but escapes its limitations. The vernacular ring to Jack's voice arises primarily from a smattering of well-codified colloquialisms: "commenced to," "a deal of," "what had" (in place of "that had"), "they was," "knowed," "them" (in place of "those"), and so on. Combined with Jack's use of natural, historically appropriate metaphors and the accuracy and specificity of his details, this technique more than masks the sophistication of Jack's narrative technique. Berger achieves great economy in his use of these colloquial code words, which, although relatively few, are well placed and impart backwoods credibility to Jack's narration without limiting the precision of either his syntax or his diction.

Jack's narration derives much of its credibility and sensory impact from its earthy figures of speech. For example, the description of the "massacre" of Jack's father's wagon train has an Indian grimacing "like he smells something stinking" and howling "like a coyote under a full moon." One of Jack's last sights of his mother has her looking "like one of them little dolls you can make out of a hollyhock blossom with a bud for its head," and Jack crosses a river on his way to Old Lodge Skins's camp holding on to the tail of a swimming pony, "spinning behind like a lure on a fishline." Other period metaphors include references to "sparks when you throw a horseshoe in the forge," to muscles that hum "like plucked bowstrings," to a sound "like when you throw a stone against a keg," and to Indians swarming across the Greasy Grass River "like bees out of a shaken hive." Some measure of the care Berger has taken in developing Jack's voice can be seen in the fact that this last simile directly echoes an actual account of the battle by a Blackfoot named Kill Eagle, whose use of that exact metaphor is singled out by Evan Connell as an example of the kind of image lacking in the writing of the white journalist who accompanied Custer.[17]

What is so remarkable is that Jack's voice rings so true, while also containing so many unexpected signs of sophistication. Included in his vocabulary are such unlikely terms as: *disjunction, recumbent, quandary, signification, obdurate, circumferentially, phenomenon, equable, cognizance, egress, colloquy, exemplify, predilection, surfeit,* and *stentorian.* His command of prepositions and adverbs alone, the careful use of directional terms such as *therewith, henceforward, thereunder, heretofore, hitherto, henceforth,* and *forthwith,* reveals considerable lexical polish. And more significant than this erudite vocabulary is the precision and rhetorical craft of many of Jack's sentences.

Consider the sophisticated, efficient, and suspensive syntax of but one of Jack's many precisely crafted and elaborately extended observations:

> As I say, none of us understood the situation, but me and Caroline was considerably better off than the chief, because we only looked to him for our upkeep in the foreseeable future, whereas he at last decided we was demons and only waiting for dark to steal the wits from his head; and while riding along he muttered prayers and incantations to bring us bad medicine, but so ran his luck that he never saw any of the animal brothers that assisted his magic—such as Rattlesnake or Prairie Dog—but rather only Jackrabbit, who had a grudge against him of longstanding because he once had kept a prairie fire off his camp by exhorting it to burn the hares' home instead. (46)

Even Ralph Fielding Snell calls attention to this phenomenon, noting that "Mr. Crabb is astonishingly circumspect as to language" and offering a strained rationale for the presence in Jack's vocabulary of such a word as "apprehension." In fact, Snell invites his readers to consider a number of specific apparent inconsistencies in Jack's narration, including the fact that while Jack's own voice is often ungrammatical, his representation of Custer's speech or of Indian discourse is always impeccable, only to conclude that "your garageman or bootblack" is equally capable of civilized rhetoric if he only wishes to do so (22–23).

Berger's game here is a complicated one: by having Snell point out the surprising flashes of apparent sophistication in Jack's narration, he puts us on our guard to the possibility that the entire narrative is a hoax; by calling attention to this verbal phenomenon, however, Snell both diverts our attention from even more unlikely aspects of Jack's voice and confirms our suspicion of his own weakness of perception. The overall effect is to bolster Jack's credibility. What should not be missed here is not the almost pro forma postmodern appearance of Berger's self-reflexivity, but the deeper questions it raises about the status of language in the Old West. For, just as surely as the interplay between the editor Snell and the narrator Crabb can only remind us of that between the editor John Ray, Jr., and the narrator Humbert Humbert in *Lolita*, the literature of the West swells with first-person narratives of astonishing sophistication. Just as Jack Crabb's voice belongs to the fraternity of metafictional voices announcing that literature is a delightful hoax, so it belongs also to the fraternity of "historical" voices determined to tell the way the Old West actually "was,"—quite different enterprises, united only by the medium of language. Profoundly, rather than superficially, realistic, Jack's voice conflates the sounds of the actual literatures of the Old West with those of the literatures of language.

Quite apart from its remarkable resonance of the specific literature of the West in the late nineteenth century, Jack's voice and character can only remind us of other voices and characters in the broader American literary tradition. Berger himself wrote of Cooper's Natty Bumppo, perhaps America's first great literary character, in terms that would apply equally well to Jack. That Berger recorded these comments in an afterword that he prepared for a 1961 edition of *The Pathfinder* and that this closely preceded or attended his writing of *Little Big Man* invites the obvious conclusion that what Berger found most interesting in Natty Bumppo found its way into the character of Jack Crabb. Any such qualities could only emerge through the fine screen of Berger's irony. But consider, for example, that Berger describes Natty as "a kind of early Margaret Mead in buckskin" who "identifies but never judges the variations among cultures."[18] (One French critic has mused of *Little Big Man*, "Perhaps Levi-Strauss would have contrived a similar story if he had been requested to write a Western dime-novel overnight.")[19]

Berger sees Natty as "an exemplar of freedom" who nevertheless "stands against anarchy," and in a clear preview of some of Jack's observations, Berger notes of Natty that "to get the better of him morally you must leave his universe altogether and consider the man who stays in the right place but cannot make a go of it—say an Indian who faints at the sight of blood, or a cowardly frontiersman."[20] Even more significantly, Berger points out that Natty "is free not to think of politics at all, a liberty unknown to any other epic hero." Not surprisingly, one of Jack's claims is simply that he "wasn't ever interested in politics" (just as unsurprisingly Berger gives the lie to this claim by having Jack consider running for public office during one of his periods of success).

Frederick Turner has written of the extensive parallels between *Little Big Man* and Melville's *Life of Israel Potter*.[21] Daniel Royot compares Jack with Ishmael in *Moby Dick* and is reminded, by Jack's impressions, of "the naturalistic lyricism of Frank Norris."[22] And while I have already noted some of the problems in comparing Jack with Huck Finn, both the first line of Jack's narrative and much in his situation call to mind *A Connecticut Yankee in King Arthur's Court*. Perhaps Berger himself best suggested the inherently American literary core of his own novel in his discussion of *The Pathfinder*:

Whenever you wish to stir up the heirs of Western civilization, put on a coonskin cap and pick up a flintlock. More than anyone else, Cooper is responsible for this image, which may be sentimental and only too easy to burlesque, as in the legend of Davy Crockett, but then all the great themes of American literature—gigantism (Melville), hysteria (Hawthorne), vulgarity (James)—are already halfway toward parody at their conception. America is that sort of place as well as the home of the wisecrack. But we must remember, too, that Crockett, for all his lies and boasts, actually did lose his life defending the Alamo. America is also the place where real life, if only in the form of real death, eventually overtakes and legitimizes invention.[23]

The Pursuit of Freedom

Although in many ways the story of Jack's narrative is itself as fascinating as, or more fascinating than, the story of his life, one aspect of that life is particularly significant, both for the ultimate meaning of *Little Big Man* and for the ultimate understanding of Berger's primary concern, in all of his novels, with the pursuit and nature of real freedom. Or, to better explain the importance of this last facet of Jack's incredible life, I should state my belief that all of the self-reflexive, metaliterary, or postmodern elements of this novel in the final analysis exist to direct our attention to the relationship between language and freedom. And it is in this light that *Little Big Man*, a literal model of a "captivity narrative," most directly dramatizes Berger's fascination with the ways in which language serves to make captives of us all.

In this one fundamental respect, Berger's contribution to the literature of the frontier strikes a radically new note. Whether by virtue of a noble primitivism, as in the case of Cooper's Leatherstocking, or by virtue of an opportunistic amorality, as in the case of most of the frontier characters of the southwestern humorists and the "wild and woolly" heroes of the Beadle dime novels, the western hero has been at bottom the very exemplar of individual freedom—often of anarchic freedom. Deadwood Dick, for example, is beyond the reach of almost all obligations because he has survived hanging as a thief. "I was cut down and resuscitated by a friend," he explains, "and thus, while I hung and paid my debt to nature and justice, I came back to life a free man whom no law in the universe could molest for past offenses."[24] In surviving the Battle of the Little Bighorn, Jack strikingly parallels Deadwood Dick's remarkable resiliency but certainly gains no sense of freedom or relief from responsibility through his escape.

What finally distinguishes Jack from his literary predecessors is that *he is not free*: he may escape the trappings of captivity, whether at the hands of the Indians, the Pendrakes, or commercial creditors, but Jack remains the slave of his own standards—his haunting sense of obligation to definitions. Jack can express admiration for his father's being "all for freedom of every type," he can credit the freed slave, Lavender, for having the "idea of real freedom," and he can acknowledge the profound instinct for freedom at the heart of Indian thinking, but Jack cannot himself escape the confinement of his own definitions. As he diagnoses his own problem when he runs away from the Pendrakes, intending to return to the Cheyenne, "God knows I thought enough about it and kept telling myself I was basically an Indian, just as when among Indians I kept seeing how I was really white to the core" (160). He may claim that "you can't get away from the fact that failure gives you a great liberty" (192) or advise, "just fall to rock bottom and you'll be a happy man" (164), but he reveals a much greater truth about his own life when he complains that "most all troubles come from having standards" (164). Jack does have standards, no matter how low his situation, but cannot reconcile the competing claims of the Cheyenne standards, which he understands and respects, with white standards—which he simply cannot keep from measuring himself against, no matter how unjustified or contradictory he knows them to be. When Jack opens his narrative with the claim "I am a white man and never forgot it," he refers to his personal curse as much as, or more than, to a matter of racial pride.

The bunco artist Allardyce T. Meriweather broaches the real root of Jack's problem when he explains to him why he, Meriweather, will employ his own sure skill as a pickpocket only in the riskier venture of preparing a con. "A man has a sense of himself, a definition," says Meriweather. "I must observe the code of my profession or I cannot live with myself" (330). Moreover, he claims that his skill as a pickpocket emerges *only* when part of a larger swindle, never for thievery alone. Meriweather's scruple parallels many seemingly contradictory Cheyenne beliefs about medicine that will or will not work, acts that are brave or shameful, conduct that is acceptable or not, and it is not in itself difficult for Jack to accept, even when it leads him to unexpected conclusions.

Indeed, Jack so intuitively feels the integrity of such a rigid adherence to definition that his feeling finally overwhelms even Jack's personal detestation of Custer. At Custer's death, Jack finally accepts his greatness, declaring, "don't let anybody ever tell you different, and if you don't agree, then maybe something is queer about your definition of greatness" (421). The reason for such an unexpected conclusion is entirely consonant with Jack's values: Custer "had worked out a style and he stuck to it" (429). Custer is great by, and true to, his own definition, and that is good enough for Jack.

The problem is that Jack's sense of himself always looks beyond the concrete satisfaction of his very real accomplishments to the impossibly abstract ideal of civilization; Jack judges himself, not as a man, but as a *white* man. Hard-nosed pragmatist or cynic in so many things, Jack is a sucker for the ideal of civilization and progress, even though he finds the reality inexorably disappointing. For him, Mrs. Pendrake emblemizes civilization, even when her actual conduct profoundly disillusions him: "She always knowed the *right thing* so far as civilization went, like an Indian knows it for savagery. . . . I fig-ured to have got the idea of white life, right then. It hadn't ought to do with the steam engine or arithmetic or even Mr. Pope's verse. Its aim was to turn out a Mrs. Pendrake" (134).

The point of all of this is that while Jack's sensibility is "beyond sentimen-tality" in most matters—and thus frequently a kind of wisdom as useful as, or more useful than, that of Old Lodge Skins—at heart it is hopelessly ro-mantic in its acceptance of the myth of progress and civilization, the myth of white culture that steamrolled the West. Intellectually, Jack is all for the In-dian concern with what *is*, as opposed to the white preoccupation with how things *should be*, but his commitment never grows firm enough to afford him any satisfaction. He simply knows too much to remain happy as an Indian, resignedly acknowledging that their way of life is perfect only "if you been born in a tent and carried on your Ma's back and lived with hocus-pocus since the day you was born and never invented the wheel" (371–72).

The one seeming exception in Jack's life proves the rule of his misery. On the night of his Indian son's birth, the night before Custer's attack on the Cheyennes camped along the Washita, Jack achieves his greatest moment of personal freedom, overcoming his white sense of morality to fulfill his Cheyenne obligation to his wife's sisters. Before making love to the three sis-ters, Jack faces his usual dilemma ("As usual, trouble lay in deciding whether I was finally white or Indian") but for once manages to suppress his "white" standards: "There could be no doubt that I had once and for all turned 100 percent Cheyenne insofar as that was possible by the actions of the body. . . . No, all seemed right to me at that moment. It was one of the few times I felt: this is the way things are and should be. I had medicine then, that's the only word for it. *I knew where the center of the world was*" (253).

Once, but not for all. The key phrase in Jack's revery is "insofar as that was possible by the actions of body," and what he fails to achieve is liberation through the actions of the mind. Custer's attack shatters his peace, destroys the world whose center he has just found, and throws him back into the clutches of white standards and expectations. Appropriately enough, the only real and lasting triumph in Jack's life must be created and measured in accordance with those standards. The triumph is his uncorrupting of the young whore, Amelia, the one hoax in his life that really succeeds, based as it is almost completely in the abstract ideals of white society and carried off al-most entirely through the medium of language.

Jack's encounter with, and subsequent "adoption" of, Amelia may be the most self-reflexive and overdetermined part of Berger's marvelously self-reflexive and overdetermined novel. In his "fathering" of Amelia, Jack inverts the pattern of his own life, in which he constantly finds and loses father figures. Amelia's abrupt transition from whoredom to high society inverts the governing principle of Jack's life, which, as he puts it, seems to be "Circumstances seemed to disintegrate upon me shortly after I had got settled in them" (275). Embedded within a structural framework that must remind us, at least in passing, of that of *Lolita* is a delightful inversion of Lolita's story: here, the older man *uncorrupts* the nymphet, making her life the measure of his devotion to bourgeois morality.

In fabricating the new Amelia, Jack most closely approaches the ideal of white society symbolized for him by Mrs. Pendrake, and his employment of all manner of disreputable means to that abstractly "pure" end may offer the best emblem of white society as it operates in Berger's novel. In this one area, Jack manages to free himself from culturally imposed definitions and to act, not as some standard of conduct dictates, but as he chooses. His explanation reveals a momentary insight into his own ever-losing struggle with absolute definitions. Acknowledging the suspect nature of Amelia's claim to be his niece, Jack defiantly states: "These considerations was not unknown to me. But look here: the kind of life I had lived, I had earned a right to say who was or wasn't my kin. Every real family I had ever possessed had been tore away from me by disaster. I got to figuring the natural relationships was jinxed for me, and when little Amelia offered herself, I accepted forthwith and believed the privilege was all mine" (343).

Tellingly enough, when Jack records his satisfaction at Amelia's success, he measures his pride in cultural rather than personal terms: "If respectability was always denied me personally, at least in this instance I was able to arrange it, so to speak, for another. That's about as high as a white man can aspire" (344).

Jack's *achievements* are Cheyenne, his *aspirations* are white, and therein lies a kind of captivity against which his shiftiness has no power. What may be the most significant of the many levels of meaning in *Little Big Man* is, not that Jack survives, but that he suffers—ever-victimized by his own hypostatization of "white" ideals. Like all of Berger's major characters, Jack displays many of the afflictions of Nietzsche's man of ressentiment, fighting and scheming for physical freedom but always hobbled by his own sense of impossible obligations. The moment of his greatest victory also reminds us of his ultimate submission to the tyranny of self-imposed definitions, just as the Indian victory at the Little Bighorn marked the end of the Plains Indian way of life.

Chapter Four

The Matter of Britain:
Arthur Rex

Q: "What is the significance of the references to the King Arthur legend
throughout the Reinhart Series?"
A: "Reinhart's quest is for the Holy Grail."
—Thomas Berger, interviewed by Douglas Hughes[1]

The Age of Chivalry Viewed
from the Time of the Cad

In language that could only be the author's, the book jacket informs us that
Arthur Rex is "Thomas Berger's salute to the age of Chivalry from his own
enmired situation in the Time of the Cad," but the insistent message of
Berger's ninth novel is that in the continuous mystery of time, the Age of
Chivalry and the "Time of the Cad" are in many ways of a piece. Running
through all distinctions between legendary past and banal present is the unity
of time, *sub specie aeternitatis* (under the aspect of eternity). As Berger's
Merlin explains to Arthur, "But, Sire, the curse which shall ruin you eventually is the selfsame which ruins all men, irrespective of their actions good or
evil, and that is Time, which is the issue of an incestuous act performed by
God on reality" (76).

Aptly described by one reviewer of *Arthur Rex* as "the Green Knight of
American fiction: a mysterious, protean outsider whose pose of destructive-
ness masks a fierce reverence for form and meaning,"[2] Berger has jokingly remarked that "the most difficult thing in life is to maintain one's belief in
one's own hoax" (6 September 1977). This most difficult of tasks constantly
falls to almost all of Berger's protagonists and, of his fifteen novels, *Arthur
Rex* most systematically explores the difficulties, dangers, and rewards of sus-
taining belief in the hoaxes both of the self and of culture. In this exploration,
Berger's presentation of Camelot has much in common with his earlier presentation of the old American West. At bottom, Jack Crabb's most serious
problems in *Little Big Man* stem precisely from his inability to hold securely

47

to his own hoax in the midst of so many others, both white and Cheyenne. If Jack is Berger's most basely democratic character, King Arthur is certainly his most nobly aristocratic, but substitute *myth* or *legend* for *hoax* and it becomes clear that in the world of Berger's writing, Jack and Arthur, king and mule skinner, share exactly the same problem: for all the events and epistemologies that roil their lives, both men are finally defined by the complex intersections of the concept of freedom with the concept of power. Appearing by turns— and often as one—in his novels as Holy Grail and fata morgana, these two most complicated hypostatizations obviously intrigue Berger, and he delights in casting them anew in his fiction.

Arthur Rex is obviously Berger's homage to Sir Thomas Malory and to the line of tellers who have made the Arthurian legend the Matter of Britain. In it Berger inevitably brings modern scrutiny and his sense of humor to the legend of King Arthur, but he does so in keeping with his self-professed "genuine hunger for gallantry and a passion for panache." And just as surely as his characters struggle to meet their own self-perceived responsibilities, this— like all of Berger's novels—reveals his own sense of responsibility to literary tradition. Indeed, Michael Malone has recorded Berger's resentment at coming across an Arthurian screenplay written by someone who had apparently read "none of Malory, Chretien de Troyes, Wolfram von Eschenbach, Alf Tennyson, Dick Wagner's *Tristan* and *Parsifal* and the many other forerunners whose works I ransacked (including two books for children which were my principal sources). . . . This unbelievable trashy practitioner," Berger exclaimed, "had *invented* his own Arthurian narrative!"[3]

Nor is Berger unmindful of his obligation to observe fundamental distinctions between the medieval mind that gave rise to these tales and the modern mind that they still engage. In his 1982 foreword to *German Medieval Tales*, Berger discussed some of these distinctions, with a particular eye toward the radical practicality evident to him in both medieval life and medieval literature. Asking his readers how, except in surface matters, we can distinguish medieval tales from the modern, Berger offers several criteria:

An immediate and not altogether droll answer might be: in *our* stories the heroes can often be easily identified as the kind of characters the reader of the Middle Ages would have thought not worth creating: the weakling, the hypochondriac, the sniveler, *et al*. Our tolerance for human frailty would probably seem to the medieval man rather the approbation for that which should be deplored. *His* hero is exemplary, even when damnable, like Dr. Faustus.

Medieval narratives are not devious in their means or uncertain in their moral focus. . . . In the Arthurian tales the reader is seldom in doubt as to the virtues, or lack thereof, of the principal figures: Sir Galahad is not secretly a rascal, nor is Mordred, underneath it all, a decent chap whose only problem consists in being misunderstood by his father the king.[4]

An unquestioning acceptance of sudden changes of fortune and a simple conviction "that the Devil will have his due" also characterize the age, he remarks, as does a robust sense of honor and a quality of ingenuous audacity.

Berger's retelling of the Arthurian legend has a double focus, at once true to the heroic essence of the myth and searching for the deeper truths beneath that heroism and its tragic end. He has indicated the complicated nature of this double focus with the observation: "We now know that greatness, wisdom, and courage are necessarily conjoined with selfishness, childishness, and petulance—had not Winston Churchill been an egomaniac, Britain would have fallen to Hitler, to give a political example. What is 'old' in the Arthurian myth is that God loves the knights of the Round Table and hates their enemies" (11 February 1977).

Or as Berger has put this dichotomy another way, "The Arthurian legend is essentially infantile: and you must understand that I believe children are naturally vicious" (2 April 1977).[5] One of Berger's most compelling characters, Gawaine, the most human and ultimately the wisest of Arthur's knights, suggests some of the effects of Berger's belief when, late in his life, he is asked by a brother if he does not long for the old days of action:

"Nay," said Sir Gawaine. "I am happy to have had them in my proper time, but of a life of adventure it can be said that there is no abiding satisfaction, for when one adventure is done, a knight liveth in expectation of another, and if the next come not soon enough he falleth in love, in the sort of love that is an adventure, for what he seeketh be the adventure and not the lovingness. And methinks this sequence is finally infantile, and beyond a certain age one can no longer be interested in games." (361)

Complexity in Camelot

In pursuing some of the adult and ironic implications of the Arthurian legend, Berger's retelling in no way diminishes the glory of Arthur's attempt or the measure of his achievement, but it does devote greater attention to the cause of the legend's final tragedy. In one sense, that tragedy centers, not on the dissolution of the Round Table nor on the estrangement of Arthur, Guinevere, and Launcelot, but on the erosion of the innocently idealistic belief that life can be governed by the simple principle of opposing good to evil.

There is a grim irony in the fact that shortly after Arthur first enunciates his principles of chivalry ("A code for, a mode of, knightly behavior, in which justice is conditioned by generosity, valor shaped by courtesy. . . . The vulgar advantage is declined. Dignity is preserved. . . . Graciousness is sought" [42].) he is constrained to kill King Ryons, the first man to hear those principles, and a king much in the mold of Uther Pendragon, Arthur's father. Reflecting on the emptiness of triumphing through the agent of an invincible sword, Arthur sees that the late Ryons may have had a point in calling chivalry "shitful rubbish" and the new king "a pompous ass of a boy" as well as a "bloody prating little preacher."

Even more portentously, while Arthur wins his first passage at arms with a king who refuses to swear fealty to him, he definitely loses his first nonviolent contest with a king who eagerly cedes all, the crafty Leodegrance: "And Arthur did marvel at the old king's cleverness, for if he accepted him as liege-subject he must needs take responsibility for him or violate the principles by which power could be exercised honorably, nay, even practically, for privilege is founded on duty, and if the horse carries the man, the animal is fed before the rider himself doth eat. Thus in certain respects the first comes last, and the greatest king is the loneliest" (73–74). Arthur's first discovery as king is that his code of chivalry inexorably subjugates him to the demands of duty, to the "many laws, ordinances, traditions, customs, and moreover, prophecies" that insure "a British king is never free to do his will" (65). "We have learnt that our father was more or less a barbarian," Arthur complains to Merlin. "But did he not have it better" (44).

That a king may not be free and that doing good may have evil consequences are but two of the many ironies of the Arthurian story, and it is those ironic notes that Berger's novel sounds again and again. Complexity finally overwhelms Arthur and even the wicked who oppose him, uniting both good and evil in the crucible of irony. Berger's narrator specifies that the tragedy of the Round Table lay, not in its dissolution, but in the cause of its fall, "for this was the only time that a king had set out to rule on principles of absolute virtue, and to fight evil and to champion the good, and though it was not the first time that a king fell out with his followers, it was unique in happening not by wicked design but rather by the helpless accidents of fine men who meant well and who loved one another dearly" (447). Only when engaged in mortal combat with his fellow knight and respected friend Gawaine does Launcelot reflect "on the differences amongst men, and how though a company of them might hold the same principles, each member might honestly interpret these in another way" (462). (Pointedly, neither narrator nor knight mentions the presence of women in the scheme of the Round Table, a blindness Berger does not allow his readers to share for long.)

Nor does complexity spare the evil, even when they try to reform. Berger's Sir Meliagrant captures and imprisons Guinevere, only to be so confounded by that "metaphysical lady" that he reluctantly renounces his evil métier in hope of winning her love. But "whereas he had been fearsome when vile, he was but a booby when he did other than ill," and his decision to reform leads in quick succession to his being robbed and wounded by a beggar, then killed in a fight with Launcelot that he knew he could not win. "This honor," muses Sir Meliagrant before his death, "can be a taxing thing" (175). In somewhat similar fashion, having had little success in her schemes against Arthur, the crafty Morgan la Fey finally enters a nunnery, "for after a long career in the service of evil she had come to believe that corruption were sooner brought amongst humankind by the forces of virtue, and from this moment on she was notable for her piety" (453).

Morgan represents one of Berger's most distinctive contributions to the legend of Arthur: giving the nature of evil intention its day in the court of myth. By giving Morgan a degree of insight that transcends her seemingly simple malevolence (she instructs Mordred, "The great purpose in doing evil is to defy the good, dear boy!"), Berger makes her an appropriately complicated inverse of Guinevere. Both women seek power, but only Morgan understands the significance of her search. When Mordred asks her whether there exists any universally observed standard, Morgan's answer reminds us that evil—as well as good—has its complexities: " 'Only,' said Morgan la Fey, 'as pertains to power, the having of which is always desirable, however obtained and for whatever uses. And oft this is a matter of great subtlety, for there are those who enjoy being victims of extreme pain. Yet a keen eye will detect that oft the true power is in the possession of the victim and not his apparent master'" (224). Mordred next asks why evil is worth doing, since like good it proves transitory. Morgan answers: "There are those of us to whom bringing pain to others is a remarkable satisfaction. . . . And do we not thereby serve Life? For only the dead are anesthetic, and whereas pleasant feelings are short-lived and never are vivid enough to escape a consciousness of the passing of Time, in the degree to which it is intense pain doth give at least the illusion of being eternal" (225).

Arthur knows when he formulates his code of chivalry that his efforts, being human, will ultimately fail, but he insists that they can fail gloriously, since glory "doth come only from a quest for that which is impossible of attainment." What he does not know is that strict adherence to a rigid code of conduct may create more problems than it solves and threaten order more than ensure it. Berger presents a humorous miniature of Arthur's profound problem in his description of Gareth's year working in the kitchens of Came-lot, where his innately noble scruples never fail to offend, or to work to the detriment of, his coworkers. Too late Gareth understands the difficulty of his situation, "that degrading oneself is a complex matter and does not necessar-ily serve the cause of modesty" (233).

A typically perverse problem Berger poses for both Arthur and his knights arises from the pride with which they define themselves precisely by the evil they oppose: in ridding the land of that evil, they call their own existence into question more than they affirm it. When the young Percival's mother chal-lenges his wish to become a knight, she observes that "for all the brave men in the world who fight for the good, there is no less of evil anywhere" (378). He can only wanly answer, "if there were no evil, then what would become of bravery?" And when Sir Percival, the most naive of knights, searches for the Holy Grail, he encounters a kind of relativity that Arthur's rule cannot as-similate. "And some of the men he met were fairly good, and some were very evil, but most were a mixture of virtues and vices whether they wore silk or rags, or lived in a palace or a hut or a cave, and taking them all in all, all were corrupt to a great degree, but none was without some small virtue, and all were equal in that they lived in Time" (419).

What dawns too slowly on Arthur and some of his knights is the realiza-tion that the code of chivalry, like any system of abstract definitions and prin-ciples, comes into conflict with itself if pursued too blindly. "To have a purpose is good," counsels the Lady of the Lake, "but to be so intent upon it as to see only its end is folly. Never to be distracted is ultimately to serve noth-ing but Vanity" (105). As philosophical as it is practical, her advice is never-theless largely lost on her knightly audience—in part, no doubt, simply because it comes from a woman, no matter how miraculous her powers or compelling her wisdom. Gawaine's honor demands that he avenge his fa-ther's death, which was at the hand of another knight, and even though that death is itself justified by the requirements of honor, Arthur sadly notes that the code's guidance begins to blur because "distinctions are sometimes hard to draw, for our obligations do oft war each on each." To Launcelot, Arthur admits that "evil doing hath got more subtle, perhaps even to the point at which it can not properly be encountered with the sword" (392).

The warring of obligations to equally compelling rationales for action fi-nally leads the two greatest of Arthur's knights, Launcelot and Gawaine, to fight each other. During that sad fight, Launcelot suddenly understands that "if Gawaine's morality were complex, it was because chivalry in general was more complicated than it seemed, for it is not easy always to know what is the noble thing, or what is brave and generous or even simply decent" (461). In Berger's hands, Arthur's most anguishing discovery is, not that he has been betrayed by his queen and his most trusted knight, but that his philosophy has been shallow. Too late comes his tragic epiphany that "to the profound vision there is no virtue and no vice, and what is justice to one, is injustice to another," a sentiment strikingly similar to Nietzsche's conceptual formula for Aeschylus's Prometheus, "All that exists is just and unjust and equally justified in both."

Despite this central flaw in Arthur's great dream, Berger makes it clear that Arthur's legend is not to be judged or reevaluated by the dream's success or failure. Nor in this or any other Berger novel should irony be mistaken for absurdity. The Lady of the Lake assures the dying Arthur that he could not have done better in his life than he did, and the ghost of Sir Gawaine offers to his king the Round Table's poignant epitaph: "we sought no easy victories, nor won any. And perhaps for that we will be remembered" (484).

The Telling of the Tale

As with all tellers of the story of King Arthur, Berger's central concern is with reminding us that while the matter of myth and the matter of history may not be the same, both may be equally true or equally false. When he describes one of his literary ancestors, Geoffrey of Monmouth, as "a shameless mythomaniac" who "was as successful as any modern statesman in fobbing off fiction as fact," Berger is not criticizing either chronicler or politician but reminding us that language has long been the most important reality (11 February 1977). The final words of Berger's narrator specify that King Arthur "was never historical, but everything he did was true," a distinction maintained in Berger's subtitling his own work *A Legendary Novel*. In Berger's view of things, the legendary should not be confused with the spurious, particularly since, as his narrator wryly observes, "it is only in the historical world that a reputation can be gained by talk alone, and in the realm of legend only deeds are counted" (427). Berger illustrates in several ways the literal application of his narrator's claim that all men of Arthur's time "lived and died by legend" and surely agrees with the conclusion that without legend "the world hath become a mean place" (433). Nevertheless, Berger steadfastly refuses to let *Arthur Rex* slip into nostalgia for a lost world of simple heroism and gallantry. Instead he urges us to contemplate the enduring complexities of the transitory joy and tragedy of the Round Table. Indeed, the paradoxes at the heart of the Arthurian legend, and the paradoxes implicit in the history of its telling, singularly well suit themselves to the worldview that emerges from all of Berger's novels, and they already constitute the kind of dialectic his writing so frequently explores.

One such dialectic has to do with Berger's writing itself, since *Arthur Rex* marks his return to material he first encountered as an eight-year-old in a children's version of *Le Morte d'Arthur*. Describing his own novel, on its bookjacket, as essentially his "memory of that childish version as edited and expanded according to the outlandish fantasies (and even some of the droll experiences) he has had in the years since," Berger touches on one of many paradoxes in the Arthurian legend: it does appeal first to the child in us, then inexorably reminds us of the world of adult consequences, a world in which the child is father to the man and not always to happy effect.

A more basic dialectic emerges from the Arthurian epistemology, which hopelessly, but perhaps profoundly, muddles its effort to dichotomize all action as good or evil, knightly or knavish. Eugene Vinaver has described the destructive conflict that finally dooms the Round Table as "the clash of the two most noble forms of love and loyalty—the blind devotion of the knight-lover to his lady and the heroic devotion of man to man. . . . The task of the novelist is to show that there is no conceivable choice between them and so to make us understand the magnitude of the drama enacted by the now familiar characters—Lancelot, Gawaine, Guinevere and Arthur—all cast for the first time in profoundly tragic parts."[6] Berger obviously agrees, even to the extent of having these four central characters be fully aware of the inescapability of their roles, but he also addresses *Arthur Rex* to the *literary* clashes inherent in the transmission of the Arthurian legend. In this sense, Berger's retelling attempts to synthesize the clash between the primacy of the concept of courtly love in earlier French versions of the tales with the primacy of Malory's allegiance to a much more male-oriented chivalric code of knightly conduct. Put another way, one of the implications of Berger's novel is that the conflict between good and evil is neither so central nor so significant to our understanding of the myth of Arthur as are somewhat less normatively charged conflicts such as that between "masculine" and "feminine" epistemologies.

And while many critics have noted the importance of the conflict between illusion and reality as a major theme in the Arthurian stories, Berger seems much more interested in this conflict at the level of telling or writing itself: his novel questions or exposes many illusions in the "events" of Arthur's world, but does so ever in pursuit of a more rigorous sense of the "reality" of that imagined world; moreover, Berger seems to believe that the application of greater rigor to the presentation of Arthur's world in no way conflicts with an ultimate allegiance to its myths. Here, as elsewhere in his novels, Berger is never contumacious toward the legendary.

Berger's agent provocateur subtly redirecting our attention toward newly understandable aspects of the Arthurian legend is, of course, his unnamed narrator—certainly Berger's most original character. It is through this narrator that Berger pays homage to Malory while refusing to make his own the limits of Malory's vision, and it is through this narrator that Berger creates, not just another version of the Arthurian story, but a comment on the traditions of its telling. This narrative voice is in many ways as distinctive and as incredible as that of Jack Crabb in *Little Big Man*, but because of its mock or quasi-omniscience, it is much more easily mistaken for the voice of its creator. The temptation to ascribe the views of this narrator to Berger himself must be resisted if the complexities of Berger's use and understanding of the Arthurian legend are to be given proper credit.

The narrator of *Arthur Rex* uniquely mirrors the dilemma of the characters in his story in that his obligations to various narrative traditions "do oft war each on each," while the panache of his prose style rivals the panache of their lives. His telling celebrates Malory and strives to be true to Malory's spirit, as well as to the larger tradition of Arthurian legend, but Berger's narrator differs from his masters in at least four major respects. Perhaps most obviously, Berger's narrator follows the conventions of Christian piety, as Malory took great pains to do, but undercuts that phatic piety with much pragmatic assessment and critique of Christianity as a system of belief. Two important corollaries to this subtle shift are that the narrator ever redirects our attention from the norms of knightly conduct to the realities of power and, while respecting the conventions of the age's conception of woman to the point of consistently "revealing" his chauvinistic subscription to that conception, even more consistently portrays the women in the Arthurian legend as the only characters deep enough and realistic enough to understand its meanings. Finally, Berger so draws his narrator as to use him, both implicitly and explicitly, as a commentator on the language and the literature of the Arthurian story.

As might be expected of a voice charged with so many tasks, Berger's narrator is a notable parenthesist, consistently incorporating both explanatory asides in his own narration and parenthetical comments in the dialogue of his characters. Perhaps only in the hands of this narrator do the characters of the Arthurian legend seem so willing to aid in the storytelling enterprise. For example, Isold, when she has only to tell Tristram that she will look for food, elaborates: "Then shall I go, . . ."for I am hale though uncombed and sans scents and fine clothes, and for the first time in my life (which began as a protected princess, after which I became a queen against my will) I may have some use" (291). In his own asides the narrator smugly, but often wisely, judges the motives of everyone from God to King Leodegrance's gardeners and heroically attempts to observe all of the hierarchical proprieties that weave and snarl the Arthurian legend. Frequently, as when he notes that only churls died from the plague and "other maladies of the common folk," while knights "did perish only in battles and ladies from love," the narrator offers tongue-in-cheek comments on Arthurian conventions, but he also balances this humorous self-reflexivity with more serious insights into the tale he tells, such as his observation that "in a strange way King Arthur and Sir Launcelot were ever reciprocal."

The narrator's very vocabulary constitutes another kind of commentary, generated by Berger's ever-present fascination with the stuff of language. A relatively small number of antique words pepper his narration, making it sound appropriate with the same efficiency a few colloquialisms made Jack Crabb's narration sound authentic. Surprisingly few of those antique usages are technical terms describing arms or dress; lances are "fewtered," castles have "machicolations," and cloth is invariably "samite" or "sendal," but the balance of the narrator's antique lexicon seems chosen for linguistic interest rather than for realistic utility. In this process *harlot* appears as a male modifier, *wench* appears as curse more than simple description, and the near-brutal pun on *queen* and *quean* is directed toward Guinevere, each use historically precise. An even more interesting phenomenon, however, lies in the narrator's use of words whose modern sense has acquired enough connotative baggage to overload root meanings (words such as *boor, villein, churl, clown,* even *furniture*) or words that have somehow been lost in modern commonplaces (*fell* has disappeared into *fell swoop, ruth* into *ruthless,* and *jade* into *jaded*). Thus, in matters philological as well as moral, Berger's narrator proves a remarkably engaging storyteller. Inherently a human construct with obvious biases and generally predictable opinions, he may not always compel our agreement, but his pronouncements consistently merit our consideration.

From the outset of Berger's novel, the narrator reveals both his essential allegiance to events as set down by Malory and his intent to establish a distinctive voice for his telling. For example, Malory takes several pages to explain the somewhat tortured sequence of events that preceded King Uther's war on the duke of Cornwall, while Berger's narrator cuts through all such preliminary explanations and rhetorical facades to the substance of the matter, specifying that substance in a single sentence: "Now Uther Pendragon, King of all Britain, conceived an inordinate passion for the fair Ygraine, duchess of Cornwall, and having otherwise no access to her, he proceeded to wage war upon her husband, Gorlois the duke" (1). Likewise, while the mere presence of the dying Uther on the battlefield is enough for Malory to explain a British victory over the Saxons, Berger's narrator, ever concerned with the powers of language, suggests that Uther's rhetoric proved more instrumental than his presence, as he "urged his host on in such words as these: 'Cut down the shit-eaters and carve their rotten bellies out and wind their stinking guts around their necks and drive staves up their dirty arseholes. Rip off their ballocks and shove them down their muzzles,' and so on in language of the greatest eloquence for its effect on the British warrior" (24).

This literal bent pervades *Arthur Rex*, even to the point of addressing the tradition that Arthur's final battle with Mordred started accidentally when a knight's drawing of his sword to kill a snake was misperceived as the breaking of a truce. Berger's narrator will not allow an accident to precipitate such an inexorable conflict and simply has Mordred treacherously run Arthur through with Excalibur. He specifies, "And so the battle began, and when the scribes say it was started by the sting of a serpent, they were not in error, for that snake was Mordred" (481).

Malory repeatedly invokes the authority of his source, noting that events proceed "as the French book sayeth." But Berger builds his narrative with only an occasional nod to "the old scribes" and with one striking acknowledgement to Malory himself, when Berger's narrator quotes what that "great knight hath written" of the possibility of Arthur's return. "Yet I woll nat say that hit shall be so, but rather I wolde sey: here in thys worlde he chaunges hys lyff" (497). Berger has obviously studied the Arthurian legend in its many variants but has no intention of following any of the older scribes. As his jacket cover note cheerfully claims, while "Mr. Berger has ransacked the work of his great predecessors . . . the further he proceeds with his own hallucinations, the more peculiarly personal becomes his narrative." What he does follow is the *example* of Malory, who drew from, mixed together, deleted, expanded on, and sometimes simply copied his own sources. And in celebrating the master's technique, Berger proves himself, if not the better teller, at least a modern maker, as his telling of the Arthurian story displays an unmistakable unity, the claimed presence or absence of which in *Le Morte d'Arthur* has been the subject of great critical debate.

Some of the terms of that debate allow us to see most clearly the significance of Berger's divergences from Malory. Charles Moorman has argued that three central narrative strands, representing three areas of knightly failure, give *Le Morte d'Arthur* precisely the unity Eugene Vinaver argued it lacks.[7] Sidestepping the Moorman-Vinaver conflict (though my sympathies lie almost entirely with the former), I would suggest that the three strands isolated by Moorman—the love of Launcelot and Guinevere, the quest for the Sangreal, and the feud between the families of Lot and Pellinore—do account for most of the action in Malory and certainly encompass his central themes. Not surprisingly, these three narrative strands also go far toward accounting for the action and themes in *Arthur Rex*, but with a significant difference. In Berger's telling, each of these three themes undergoes considerable alterations that subtly but surely displace its emphasis. Berger's approach to the story of Launcelot and Guinevere is to recast it outside the conventions of courtly love, making it one of several investigations of the relationship between man and woman. Indeed, while Berger accords dramatic primacy to the relationship between Launcelot and Guinevere, he clearly shifts philosophical primacy to Gawaine's relationships with women, most notably Lady Ragnell. Likewise, Berger's narrative displaces emphasis from the spiritual significance of the quest for the Sangreal to the philosophical significance of the general quest for power and the necessarily related quest for understanding. Finally, while Berger retains all of the stages in the feud between the houses of Lot and Pellinore, he widens the scope of that conflict to encompass the more basic conflict between human variability and hierarchical rigidity—his ever present acknowledgment of the complexity of life.

One of the clearest results of these subtle shifts of emphasis is that for all the pro forma declarations of the primacy of Launcelot, Gawaine emerges as Berger's "best" knight. In the Arthurian catalog of superlative qualities, Gawaine appears to offer a kind of golden mean. As the Green Knight explains to Gawaine, "To be greater than you is to be tragic; to be less, farcical" (214). And it is one of Berger's characteristic ironies that his version of the Arthurian legend has the two greatest knights fight to the death, Launcelot prevailing in arms even as he begins to understand that Gawaine has bettered him in understanding.

Whatever his declarations that seem to support a medieval worldview, Berger's narrator also acknowledges the existence of a modern perspective influenced by the secular arguments of Nietzsche and Freud. While Arthur's knights live and die measuring their manly worth on the abstract scale of puissance, Berger's narrator inexorably shifts the focus of *Arthur Rex* to the vagaries of power, a sexless phenomenon that, unlike puissance, must have an object upon which to act. An equally modern concern for formal unity also emerges from Berger's recombinations of knightly tales, adopting, as it seems, the circularity of the Round Table as the governing principle for structuring its story. To this end, in Berger's telling, the conflict between fathers and sons becomes a central recurring principle, as do doomed lovers' triangles and the complexities of the calculus of power. Indeed, the question of power as manifested in all manner of medieval relations may lie at the very heart of *Arthur Rex*, with particular significance for Berger's presentation of relations between the sexes and for his presentation of the phenomenon of medieval Christianity.

While never directly challenging the tenets of medieval theology, for example, Berger's narrator consistently opts for presenting Arthur's story as a human as well as, or even rather than, Christian allegory. Perhaps the secularizing tendency (itself an extension, rather than refutation, of the thrust of Malory's telling) most clearly appears in the use Berger makes of the quest for the Sangreal. In his telling, that quest emerges as more an expedient for maintaining the spirit of the Round Table in the absence of virtuous wars than as a measure of spiritual perfection: more than a Snark hunt, it is less than the test of the Round Table. Significantly enough, Arthur first learns of the quest for the Grail from the wily King Leodegrance and notes some puzzlement that none of his clerics, and not even Launcelot, his most devout knight, are familiar with the concept. In Berger's hands, this quest becomes emblematic of the genius of the Arthurian enterprise ("an admirable ideal: to quest for that of which the precise nature were unknown, yet holy in the large" [302]), rather than for failure, foreshadowing the fall of the Round Table itself. The most obvious result of this changed emphasis is that Berger's Galahad must have purpose apart from achieving the Grail, and in making a sickly Galahad the accidental slayer of Launcelot, Berger completes his redirection of our attention from the Sangreal to more human dramas.

More directly, Merlin, a Nietzschean rather than a Machiavellian, furnishes Berger a most convenient means of assessing Christian belief without necessarily questioning it, since, as the narrator explains in one of his pervasive parentheses, Merlin, while not himself a Christian, "did believe that faith furnished a shape to the amorphous existence of men and an oriflamme to follow that did not so quickly tatter as those of mortal reigns" (27). Merlin's concern with the Church is political rather than spiritual, and he offers his views to Arthur so the young king might "see power clearly." "As an institution," suggests Merlin, "Christianity doth provide a containment for the mob as the banks of a stream a channel for the water, and as a faith it doth meet the universal requirement of men for that which is beyond the evident, the which is often vile. And the Nazarene, by taking upon himself the guilt for all human pollution, hath proved the most cunning god of the many to which mortals have resorted" (34). (Arthur, of course, rejects this view as blasphemous and declares: "I shall be a Christian king because Christ was Our Saviour, and not because of expediency, political or spiritual.")

In their respective approaches to Christianity, as in most matters, Merlin and Arthur reveal strengths so different as to be incommensurate. Amused by Arthur's persistent deflation of the myth surrounding Excalibur, Merlin cautions: "I am a wizard and not a logician, as you are a king and not a philosopher. Any effort to compound these offices is inadvisable" (38).

This exchange is characteristic, in several important ways, of Berger's approach in *Arthur Rex*. While revealing that Arthur is not a philosopher—in Merlin's somewhat narrowly drawn terms—it also shows him as anything but the cutely simple Wart of White's *Once and Future King*. In attempting to understand his life and to understand the unfolding legend that more and more envelops it, Arthur questions the precise meaning of the Excalibur part of his legend on a linguistically literal level, and is not content with accepting the curse of "invincibility" without exploring it, as does Launcelot. And it is through just this sort of questioning that Berger's Arthur and Gawaine distinguish themselves from other members of the Round Table. Reminded by Arthur that "it is written" that Launcelot cannot be overcome, Gawaine even dares to question the "rules" of legend, defiantly asking: "Where? . . . and by whom? Some lily livered scribe who hath never held a sword? Some romancer who would confine us to a myth?" (445). As so often proves the case in Berger's fiction, definitions become destiny: Arthur is a king, not a philosopher; Merlin is a wizard, not a logician; and Gawaine is doomed by myth never to overcome Launcelot. For Gawaine and Arthur and Merlin, however, these definitions are imposed by the Arthurian legend rather than by any bent toward self-victimization.

"I am interested only in that which is mythical," the Lady of the Lake explains to Merlin, rejecting his seeming miracles as the mere "physical application of reason" (107). And so, in a sense, is Berger. *Arthur Rex* shows forth again and again, however, its author's determination to chart precisely the territory of the mythical, understanding its mechanisms and rigorously tightening its description, and to this end Berger draws Merlin as more of a disturbing devil's advocate than as avuncular guide and offers in Merlin's conversations with Arthur, and Arthur's with Gawaine, the positive lessons of Arthur's noble experiment.

More oblique lessons emerge from Berger's presentation of medieval theology. What Berger's narrator identifies as Merlin's "unique sense of irony, quite foreign to the mortals of that straightforward time," actually proves more charitable toward Christianity than the narrator's own ostensibly pious attempts to rationalize its mortal consequences. Always at pains to offer at least the age's explanation of God's ways, the narrator pursues his rationales to their ironic conclusions, as when he describes Galahad: "Thus Galahad was to be the one perfect knight, for God doth allow perfection only to him who is already dying, and even the most evil of men acquire more virtue with each of their final breaths, and no doubt God doth cure us all by killing us in the end" (425).

Displaying her own perverse wisdom, Morgan la Fey instructs Mordred in using love as torture, concluding, "The cunning device of the Christian religion is to maintain that love bringeth joy, while it is precisely the reverse which is true: that love doth bring only agony to the lover" (222). Merlin and Guinevere both point out to Arthur disparities between the state of nature and his interpretation of Christian dogma, and Tristan's simple conviction that Isold was intended by God to be a queen forces Tristan to abandon their actual idyllic life together in the woods to return to the courtly life idealized in the manically hierarchical schema of medieval Christian belief. One of the inescapable and radical implications of Berger's novel is that the Round Table falls, not simply because the Christian view of human imperfectability requires it to, but at least in part because its principle of circularity is so inherently at odds with the linear hierarchies of medieval Christian thought. "A circle can never be put to the hierarchical uses of a rectangle, turning each corner of which is, in a sense, a moral event," explains Arthur when he asks Leodegrance for the Round Table.[8] Arthur's design, however, almost immediately falls victim to the concept it sought to thwart: Pellinore sits on Arthur's left hand because he also is a king, and the seat on Arthur's right, the Siege Perilous, is reserved for "the Perfect Knight," whose coming will spell the end of the Round Table. The iconography of the Round Table precludes some ills but, like Arthur's reign itself, cannot supplant all old difficulties. By far the more telling icon is that of the golden chains—reminders of the great chain of being as well as of the king's captivity to his throne—which appear to Arthur in a dream portending the inevitable slide of his rule into chaos.

Abstract hierarchies rest on absolute definitions—always a problem in Berger's fiction. "God, and not men, establishes all hierarchies," declares the ostentatiously pious Launcelot, unwittingly specifying the concept that insures his own doom. Hierarchical thinking receives much attention from Berger's narrator, usually to humorous effect. Indeed, apart from references to the casual cruelty of medieval thought and action, the narrator relies most heavily on the drawing of hierarchical distinctions to characterize the spirit of Arthur's age.

In a cast of superlative knights and most beautiful ladies, such distinctions grow humorously difficult to maintain. Thus in Arthur's final battle the exploits of two of his greatest knights, Launcelot and Percival, must be meticulously charted to measure the fine difference in their excellence: using only his left arm, Lancelot slew two hundred men of Cornwall, while Percival "did kill an hundred ninety-nine of these enemy and he wounded one mortally, who died within half an hour" (473). Beauty, too, has its hierarchies to be rigidly maintained, as we learn when told that Elaine of Astolat "was (now that Isold had been married) the most beautiful maiden in the world," while Isold and Guinevere "were never to be compared side by side, but the latter was the greater beauty because her hair was of the color of gold, the most precious substance on earth, for which all men search and many die" (131). Such drawing of ever finer distinctions highlights a similar tendency in Malory, who reports in one passage that the sunbeam attending the appearance of the Grail was "more clearer by seven times" than any seen before, but, more important, this preoccupation with comparative rank and merit establishes the difficulty inherent in trying to maintain relatively concrete hierarchies, a difficulty leading to tragic consequences in more abstract issues such as loyalty and love.

Central to the problem of hierarchical thinking, as well as central to the events in Berger's telling, is the blindness of Arthurian men to the wisdom of Arthurian women, "for not even Merlin, with all his arts, could divine the ways of women." But Berger relates this seeming mystery to the also misunderstood nature of power in general. One of the most poignantly revealing moments in the novel comes when Arthur grumbles to Launcelot about the inscrutability of the Lady of the Lake, referred to by the king as "that woman."

> "Tell me, Launcelot, art thou truly at ease with any female?"
> "Sire, I am not," said Sir Launcelot.
> "Dost understand them at all?" asked King Arthur.
> And Launcelot said, "Nay, I do not." (304)

Berger has claimed that in *Arthur Rex*, "perhaps for the first time since Marie de France, the queens and princesses are permitted their due in the tales, of which they are the traditional survivors; and as Launcelot, invincible on the field, must defer to Guinevere in the boudoir, so must Tristram be shown as the helpless sex-object of two Isolds."

Even more significant in this respect is the emphasis Berger gives to the tutoring of Gawaine by the Lady of the Lake, which culminates in his finest and most philosophical act—his marriage to, and subsequent acknowledgment of the free will of, Lady Ragnell. "Thou art not an object which I possess like unto a suit of armor," reasons Gawaine. "Thou art one of God's creatures, and in all fundamental matters thou must answer only to Him" (325). Her enchantment broken precisely by his refusal to exercise a power over her that is clearly granted him by the hierarchical schema of their time, Lady Ragnell calls attention to one of the many ironies implicit in Berger's presentation, explaining to Gawaine, "And in allowing me mine own choice, thou hast liberated me in more ways than one" (326). In embedding "The Wedding of Sir Gawaine and Dame Ragnell" in his Arthurian story, Berger most clearly rejects Malory's depiction of Gawaine and the simple chauvinism of most medieval narratives, for despite the perfunctory condescension of his narrator ("And so with females, of whom the wise man saith, *Turn them upside down, they do look much the same*"), Berger's women are by far the most interesting characters in *Arthur Rex*, and his most wise. In their reaction to the world around them lies a sure sign that the sensibility behind what has been persuasively called "the Arthur book for our time" is that of Thomas Berger.[9]

Chapter Five

Subversions of Good Order: *Killing Time, Regiment of Women, Who Is Teddy Villanova?*, and *Nowhere*

> For the inconsistencies in the book, and I am aware that there are not a few, I must ask the indulgence of the reader. The blame, however, lies chiefly with the Erewhonians themselves, for they were really a very difficult people to understand.
>
> —Samuel Butler, preface to the second edition of *Erewhon*[1]

The cartographers of recent literature and criticism have taken great pains to remind us that the precise location of all fiction is nowhere, that what we refer to as the setting of a piece of fiction, or its "semblance," is no less an illusory construct of language and imagination than are its characters and the events in their lives that form their story. Likewise, the chroniclers of fantastic lands in fiction, writers such as Swift, Butler, and Borges, have suggested nothing so strongly as that the people in their imaginary realms are inconsistent and difficult to understand, no more and no less than are we ourselves. Thus the discovery of the real within the fantastic has been the primary game of the literary tradition that includes *Gulliver's Travels* and *Erewhon*, a tradition extended with a twist or two by Berger to *Nowhere*, a novel that suggests the hardiness of banality in even the most wondrous terrain.

In fact, *Nowhere*, the title of Berger's thirteenth novel, is the exact setting of all of his fiction, no matter how real or historical the world of particular novels such as *Little Big Man* or *Sneaky People* may seem to be. And the inconsistency of the inhabitants of Saint Sebastian is no more remarkable, indeed no less paratactic, than that which characters display in Berger's other novels or that which they attribute to "real" places, such as the Old West or current day New York City. Some of Berger's novels, however, develop semblances so paratactically structured as to seem fantastic even within the exuberant range of his imagination. *Killing Time, Regiment of Women, Who Is*

Teddy Villanova?, and *Nowhere* each present fictional worlds that so defy our expectations of cultural and literary order that they perversely challenge, complicate, or turn upside down many of the received ideas held most dear by our culture and its literary traditions. In these four novels, delightfully odd even in Berger's canon, his paratactic technique is most relentlessly employed and therefore most easily seen. As opposed to *Little Big Man* and *Arthur Rex*, where Berger's characteristically unexpected combinations of language or sensibility occur *within* a well established literary code, these novels erect their semblances from the paratactic clash *among* competing and sometimes seemingly incompatible literary traditions and codes. These are novels that open in one genre only to switch to another and then a third, and so on until the reader has been disabused of all expectations concerning human and literary behavior. Through this parataxis of literary structures, Berger arrives at novels that achieve independent existence by overloading and overcomplicating our received notions of genre, layering conflicting arrangements of plot, characterization, and prose style in such a way as to radically expose and deconstruct the layers of literary expectations we bring to the reading of a novel.

Killing Time

If books can be said to have personalities, this novel, Berger's fourth, subtly unfolds a personality as seductively psychopathic as that of its central figure, Joe Detweiler. The disarmingly innocent and considerate Detweiler happens to be a mass murderer who often sounds like a crazed general semanticist. And the act of reading this novel involves the reader in what a psychology text might label "egocentric and antisocial activity which tends to blur perception of social and moral obligations." In short, this novel, like its central figure, kills more than time.

Each of Berger's celebrations of a literary genre is, as he has noted, also "effectively a funeral sermon" for that genre. Berger explains: "By using one of these genres as my own, I murder it—for myself. Or, if you like, I consume it. Once its nutritive cells have become part of my own flesh, I go on to devour something else" (16 September 1977). Behind this cannibalistic rhetoric lies the fact that *Killing Time* is murder on genre frames, invoking then frustrating one set of genre expectations after another in something of a paratactic merry-go-round of literary conventions. Indeed, appearing as it did on the heels of the more exuberantly written *Reinhart in Love* and *Little Big Man*, *Killing Time* was the first of Berger's novels to so frustrate expectations as to be taxed for its originality.

The novel's action (*inaction* might be more accurate) begins with the Christmas Eve discovery by a young woman, Betty Bayson, that her mother and her nude-model sister have been strangled and that the male roomer in their apartment has a screwdriver planted in his temple. All seems in order for a murder mystery as the police investigative machinery goes into action and we are made privy to the interrogative philosophy and initial suspicions of Lieutenant Shuster and Detective Tierney. Joe, the murderer, however, turns himself in even before their suspicions begin to crystallize, an act, on his part, of simple courtesy toward the hardworking cops. "It makes me feel lousy to keep them in suspense, taking up their time with a problem I could very easily settle" (160). The balance of the novel then focuses on the murderer's conversations with the police, with journalists, and with his lawyer, a brilliant strategist and rhetorician named Henry Webster Melrose, whose propositions about the courtroom ("Reality is what the jury believes") clearly parallel those of Berger the novelist. Indeed, when Melrose notes Joe's ability to "maneuver the other fellow into taking what should be your side of the argument, and you take his" (255), he also describes a persistent strategy of almost all Berger's protagonists, perhaps even of the writer himself.

Melrose's considerable legal prowess is prominently displayed by Berger, and Joe Detweiler inevitably reminds us of Leopold and Loeb, but *Killing Time* declines to become a courtroom drama. Instead its story develops through a paratactic maze of formula patterns from police procedural, psychological thriller, sensational journalism, and psychiatric case studies. Just as Joe spends most of the novel talking to others, the novel spends most of its time ranging through the "talk," or language codes, usually associated with other novel forms or with altogether other forms of discourse.

As its title also makes clear, *Killing Time* is a novel each of whose characters must relate to the usually distressing phenomenon of time, itself another significant concern throughout Berger's fiction. Believing that time is continuous rather than linear, Joe pursues the goal of "Realization," a kind of time travel of consciousness that sounds transcendental. His particular goal is to reexperience in its fullness a prior moment in time. When at last he succeeds during his own murder trial, (others take his reaction as a sure sign of his madness), the moment he completely recaptures is, ironically, that of Daniel M'Naghten's 1843 trial in London for the murder of Sir Robert Peel's secretary. Even though there is no advantage in shifting his consciousness into that of another prisoner on trial for murder, a shift at any rate only momentary, Joe finds in it joyous confirmation of his philosophy. One of the reasons Joe feels that his killing of three people is a matter of no great importance is his confidence that if he can recover the reality of the past, he can recall those he has killed—since all he has taken from them is time. Joe's radiant philosophy supplies Berger's novel with an elaborate inversion of the accepted notion of killing time. Opposed to the common sense of passing the unimportant time between significant events, Joe presents killing time as the achievement of mastery, a freeing of oneself from time's grasp. The joke, of course, is that this sure sign of his madness is no less than the implicit goal of every character in the novel.

Some of the jumbling of philosophical, narrative, and linguistic codes in this novel can be accounted for in its peculiar genesis, since, in setting out to write in one literary code (that of the "true crime documentary"), Berger drew much of his information from works in two quite different and nonliterary codes: Quentin Reynold's *Courtroom* (1951) and Frederic Wertham's *Show of Violence* (1949).[2] Both "nonfiction" works purport to tell the story of Robert Irwin, "the gentle killer." Reynolds, however, is interested in Irwin only insofar as he provided the lawyer Samuel Leibowitz, the subject of *Courtroom* and the real-life model for Berger's Melrose, with an interesting and challenging case. A psychiatrist with a knack for being in the public eye, Frederick Wertham included Irwin in his *Show of Violence* because Irwin had been one of his patients, both before and after his murder of three people. Apart from supplying the basic details of Berger's novel, these two nonfictional works provide in themselves exactly the kind of conflicting language codes that Berger focused on in *Little Big Man*, and, as Berger has specified, they raise questions about the distinctions we normally draw between fact and fiction:

Wertham's book as I remember was of little use to me, though you may well find details in it that I used and do not recall. Reynolds's account on the other hand was exactly the journalistic kind of thing that provided me with what I needed for my fiction.

Of course, when you pursue the matter of the associations between fact and fiction you must not fail to consider that what Reynolds writes is not necessarily "fact." The Irwin of *Courtroom* is an altogether different person from that of Wertham's book, in my judgment; and it should not astonish me to find that Detweiler is more like the patient in Dannemora than either. My Uffizi admonition to the reader was intended to suggest, in my usual convoluted manner, that fiction is not to be confused with life, because the *latter* is false. (27 June 1976)

The admonition to which Berger refers appeared as the frontispiece to his novel: "Readers are earnestly advised not to identify the characters in the narrative which follows—criminals, policemen, madmen, citizens, or any combination thereof—with real human beings. A work of fiction is a construction of language and otherwise a lie. Some years ago a notice was posted at the entrance to Sala B of the Uffizi Gallery in Florence: 'Please don't touch the pictures! It is dangerous for the works of art, it is punished by law, and finally it is useless.' " Having explicitly urged us to consider that "a work of fiction is a construction of language and otherwise a lie," Berger confronts us with a novel so paratactically constructed as to render that message virtually inescapable—yet irrelevant. The "lie" of *Killing Time* both closely parallels the "truth" of other accounts of Irwin's murders and subsequent trial and, more important, lays bare the linguistic and conceptual mechanics that structure the lies of fiction and the truths of fact, revealing them to be indistinguishable.

Killing Time casts police detectives, reporters, newspaper editors, lawyers, psychiatrists, and random citizens as conscious and unconscious fiction-makers who manipulate (and even more are manipulated by) the expectation patterns their fictions create. As a matter of fact, the psychopathic Joe Detweiler is the only character not involved in this process, perhaps because as a madman he has already broken through what Berger seems to see as the chimerical distinction between fiction and reality. Joe is probably the only character in the novel (Melrose might be another) truly capable of understanding that a work of fiction is a construction of language, as is much of what passes for reality.

Unmistakably a madman (he believes "everybody was habitually pretty nice to everybody else"), even within the self-consuming context of Berger's irony, Joe is himself something of a compendium of Berger's characteristic parataxis, as he must remind us not only of Leopold and Loeb but of Jesus Christ, Bartleby the scrivener, Alfred Korzybski, Emerson, and Thoreau. A uniquely altruistic Nietzschean, Joe—like Reinhart before him—believes in the fundamental immorality of sympathy but has worked out a rigorous scheme for helping people by having them befriend him:

In a crowded subway car, for example, he would pretend to be lame. It was gratifying to see the seated passengers as he limped on board, contesting with one another to claim the power he had made available. Detweiler understood that this state of affairs must be depressing to the truly disabled, and therefore he himself made it a practice never to do a favor for a cripple, but rather to ask a kindness. He would collide with a blindman, saying, "Excuse me, I am blind." Always the individual concerned would lead him to a seat, guide him across an intersection, and, of special interest to Detweiler, would often conceal his own disability. That is, would believe he was concealing it, which did him a world of good. For a few moments, anyway, he was not blind, for experience is the interaction of contrasts. (22)

In fact, apart from scattered exceptions, including mass murder, Joe does bring out the best in those around him. What he reflects, however, is not the same as what he reflects upon: his life pursues one philosophy while illustrating another, that of Berger, his creator. Joe's concern is with what he calls "Realization," a project for discarding language and any other abstract system that mediates the direct experience of reality. Committed to direct experience, Joe has absolutely no use for "men who deal in language," insisting that all they "are talking about is talk."

Joe's contention that language is basically a hoax is but one aspect of this novel that self-reflexively announces that *Killing Time* is no less a hoax than any of the many it contains. Over and over, Berger has Joe's story involve characters whose verbal deceptions and sense of artistry are obviously resonant with those used by the novelist (one character even responds to the events of the novel by becoming a novelist). Moreover, Berger also places his characters in situation after situation in which they must—like readers of the novel in which they appear—"read" the selfishly crafted words of those around them. Perhaps Berger's Melrose best suggests the working of this technique when he admits that "nothing gave him more gratification than a favorable verdict returned by a jury who knew it had been hoaxed" (197). The parallel to the relationship between novelist and reader is hard to miss.

Regiment of Women

Killing Time explores the paradox of a madman's making more sense than does the supposedly sane society that condemns him; *Regiment of Women* reverses the pattern to explore the paradox of a sane man trapped in a society that seems mad but whose madness—made to seem ludicrous in practice—remains distressingly plausible, if not familiar, in theory. The year 1972 saw the birth of the more or less official voice of the women's liberation movement, *Ms.* magazine. In that year the insistent concerns of the women's movement were raised even in the chauvinist bastion of *Esquire*, "The Magazine for Men," where Nora Ephron devoted columns to feminist issues, such as "Breasts" and "Is There Sex after Liberation." In April 1972 *Esquire* also began a column carrying Thomas Berger's musings about current films, and Berger immediately involved himself in the marginalia of the women's movement with a column devoted to Andy Warhol's two films *Some of My Best Friends Are . . .* and *Sex*. What emerges from Berger's account is his fascination with the girlish virtues of Candy Darling, Warhol's transvestite hero/heroine:

But even when bare-chested and, divested of her wig, close-cropped, Candy is still somehow all girl. A vulnerable maiden being brutalized by a sadistic male. This may be why the scene is actually very moving, in more ways than one, *naturlich-mein Herr*—but to put kinkiness aside for a moment, if that can be done when talking about, my God, a man who is girlier than many contemporary women, what one feels most here is the old moral shock of seeing an imposter, in whatever realm, unmasked. Reality, which is to say the injustice of Nature, wins again.[3]

I mention all this because in 1972 Thomas Berger was putting the finishing touches on his sixth novel, *Regiment of Women*, a book that seems very much concerned with the vagaries of sexual roles and the unmasking of imposters as it pursues Berger's deeper concerns with the nature of individuality and freedom. It is a novel anticipated by Berger's comments about Candy Darling, for in it "reality wins again" as the "injustice of Nature" proves stronger than the injustice of language—specifically the rhetoric of sexuality.

The novel presents a distressing view of a dystopian American society in 2047, where male and female roles, as they were broadly stereotyped at the time of Berger's writing, have been completely reversed. Not only do women control the corporate, artistic, legal, and military machinery of this society (although the control is sloppy and the society seedy) but they sexually dominate, strapping dildos over their pants to assault men. Naturally enough in such a world, failure to experience anal orgasm is the ultimate shame for any man. "Normal" sex is not only proscribed but unremembered, as huge birth facilities produce babies in artificial wombs with sperm collected by milking machines in Sperm Service camps. Men are drafted to serve short terms in these camps, while women fight the wars. To be manly is to wear dresses and makeup, to hold only powerless jobs, to have silicone breast implants, and to be emotionally incapable of rational thought or significant action. To be effeminate is to bind breasts, to wear false beards, to dress in pants, suits, etc., to be rough, physical, aggressive, and to have a reduced life expectancy due to the stress of responsibilities. More important, women control both definition and history: to be male is to be inferior, as is witnessed by the history of achievements such as Leonarda's "Mono Liso," works by Thomasina Gainsborough, and even "The Rape of the Sabine Men." Described in this fashion, *Regiment of Women* seems to offer little more than topical gimmickry carried to outlandish lengths, a single joke carried too far. Even Berger's comments about the book encourage such a view as he claims: "*Regiment of Women* is simply my fantasy of what would surely happen if the tables were truly turned. It is a utopian-pastoral-anatomical romance, nothing more. My work is never tendentious, and therefore still less hortatory."[4]

This disclaimer notwithstanding, *Regiment of Women* appears tendentious with a gleeful vengeance—as initial reviewers were quick to note. The fascinating point, however, is that those reviewers could not agree on the direction of Berger's bias. A sampling of their comments yields perplexingly contradictory assessments. Richard Todd began his *Atlantic* review with the suspicion that "certain feminist simplicities seem to have gotten to Thomas Berger," and he felt that the book mercilessly spoofed "radical feminists by imitating and hyperbolizing their vision of society with reversed roles."[5] Reviewers in *Psychology Today, Virginia Quarterly Review,* and the *Times Literary Supplement* echoed Todd's reading.[6] Yet Lore Dickstein, reviewing the novel for *Ms.,* found nothing to offend "those of us serious about sexual politics."[7] Claiming that to read the book solely as a comment on women's liberation or on male chauvinism was to underestimate Berger's "irresponsibility" (an application of this term in a way I believe Berger would welcome), Dickstein explained that "true to form, Berger spares no one," his "anarchic imagination exaggerat[ing] all sexual stereotypes into ludicrous postures, perhaps to show how they rob us of our freedom."[8]

Leo Braudy also aligned himself with the reviewers who refused to read *Regiment of Women* as a sexual polemic, suggesting that Berger's refusal to allow the reader the comfort of alliance with the author ("us") against a clearly wrongheaded "them" was a scathing sign of the writer's integrity.[9] Walter Clemons, however, writing in *Newsweek,* reached an astonishingly different conclusion, advising his readers that the misadventures of Berger's protagonist, Georgie Cornell, "turn the tables on all male-chauvinist readers more effectively than the most eloquent women's lib manifesto."[10] Other reviewers located themselves in various places along the interpretive continuum represented by Todd, Dickstein, Braudy, and Clemons; while they could not agree on exactly what Berger was up to, they uniformly discussed *Regiment of Women* as a novel whose main concern was with sexuality and sexual stereotyping.

My purpose in citing these amazingly disparate responses is not just to suggest the vagaries of book reviewing (although any examination of Berger's career would certainly fuel such a suggestion) but to remind critical readers that the topical surfaces of Berger's fiction should not blind us to its deeper philosophical preoccupation with the hypostatizing power of language. What *Regiment of Women* so insidiously does is seduce us with its ostensible kinkiness into gradually realizing that all of its sexual vagaries stem from the even more profound vagaries of the relationship between word and object.

At the bottom of this concern with language lies Berger's belief that victimization in any realm starts as, and often remains, primarily a linguistic phenomenon in which the generalizations and attendant rhetoric of some self-interest part company with the particulars of immediate experience. A close reading of *Regiment of Women* reveals such a focus on the workings of language and discloses so many self-reflexive or decomposing aspects of its narrative that it becomes apparent that the state of society and the state of sexual equality are of only incidental interest to Berger, who is after far bigger game.

Berger's protagonist in his inverted future world is a twenty-nine-year-old, insecurity-riddled male secretary named Georgie Cornell. Like each Berger protagonist, Georgie struggles to free himself from the inexorable tendency to think of himself as a victim of outrages and impositions, both humorously small and tragically large. Almost never in control of the situation around him, Georgie consistently finds himself outmaneuvered, outsmarted, insulted, and imposed upon. Only when he begins to realize how language has been used to distort his sense of reality does Georgie move toward individuality and freedom.

Leo Braudy has correctly suggested that Berger's concern is "with the way language can falsify reality" and that *Regiment of Women* "indicts the society that uses language as a tool of oppression, making purely verbal differences into codes and categories—rhetoric asserting and experiencing itself as 'truth.'"[11] Berger indicts, however, only insofar as he reveals, and his revelations apply to *all* uses of language—including those of the novelist. What *Regiment of Women* examines is, not sexual roles, but the more basic problem spelled out by Georgie's female companion when she muses, "Suppose everything you've been told all your life is a lot of shit."

To the end of discovering his individuality, Georgie must supplant a vocabulary of received ideas with the knowledge of his own experience. He finally understands of all his acquaintances:

The lieutenant was obsessed with her project—as Stanley and the men of the movement had been with theirs; and Harriet with hers. Cornell never had a *personal* association with anyone. Everyone he encountered was a monomaniac of some sort, working compulsively to affect someone else: to alter their personality, change their mind, catch them out, set them straight. Everybody else always *knew better* about sex, society, history, you name it—but always in a general way, with no acknowledgment of one single, particular, individual human being; by which he meant himself. (215)

Characteristically, Berger refuses to be another person who *knows better*, although the implication is clear that he sees this as a phenomenon not limited to fictive worlds.

Furthermore, Berger deliberately confuses the distinction between the wrongheadedly manipulative rhetoric of this fictive society and the "natural" rhetoric of his readers' world by reminding us with "factual"(historical) quotations before each chapter that the rhetoric of our reality has often been no less outrageous, no less shamelessly manipulative. The first of these "natural" quotations comes from the religious reformer John Knox's "First Blast of the Trumpet Against the Monstrous Regiment of Women" and highlights both Berger's reflexive technique and its effect. "To promote a woman to bear rule, superiority, dominion, or empire above any realm, nation, or city, is repugnant to nature; contumely to God, a thing most contrarious to His revealed will and approved ordinances; and finally, it is the subversion of good order, of all equity and justice."

Language like this should quickly remind us that "good order," "equity," and "justice" are, to a great extent, linguistic constructs—fictions built by the arbitrary use of language just as surely as, and often more selfishly than, is the fictional world of a novel. In this sense, *Regiment of Women* cheerfully goes about subverting good order by highlighting the double-edged, referent-free nature of its reifying rhetoric. Over and over, Berger's choice of quotations to introduce his chapters reminds us that the unnatural values of his fictive world are essentially no different from many natural values in the world of his readers. Berger assembles a collection of male chauvinist polemics, from Aristotle to Grover Cleveland, drawing on the authority of *the Bible, the Koran,* Confucius, and other theologians and philosophers. However, he increasingly intersperses these patriarchal thunderings with quotations sympathetic to the plight of women—comments by Montaigne, John Stuart Mill, Christabel Pankhurst, Olive Schreiner, and Virginia Woolf. Accordingly, the progression of quotations before each chapter roughly parallels the progression of Georgie's search for identity. Appropriately enough, Berger ends the implicit dialectic between opposed rhetorics with Nietzsche's synthesizing view that "woman was God's *second* mistake."

That *Regiment of Women* packs considerable sexual affective impact cannot be denied, but Berger's primary concern is, not with sex, but with power, and in Berger's novels power is almost always a function of language. With Nietzsche (whose importance for Berger cannot be noted too frequently),

Berger believes that "there are higher problems than the problems of pleasure and pain and sympathy," though few of Berger's characters (and least of all Georgie) would subscribe to this view. What Georgie doesn't quite realize, but what Berger surely does and his readers may, is that the particularity of experience does not have to be opposed to the generality of language and that the workings of language must be understood, however, if it is to serve the interest of individual freedom—whether of a novel's character, its author, or its reader.

Who Is Teddy Villanova?

Particularly in the wake of considering such a seemingly topical novel as *Regiment of Women*, it must not be forgotten that Berger writes novels for fun—to amuse himself with the vagaries and felicities of language—rather than to advance a program of social conduct, to criticize his society, or to turn the novel in a new direction. Which is to say that the bizarre syntax of prose styles in *Who Is Teddy Villanova?* can probably best be explained simply as something the crafting of which gave its author great pleasure. Certainly Berger must have enjoyed writing this book, using its ostensible plot as an excuse for creating some of the most striking individual sentences in all of his fiction.

That, of course, is saying a lot, since, sentence by sentence, the novels of Thomas Berger are among the most precisely crafted in the English language. He is quick to acknowledge and to elaborate his fascination with this basic unit of prose style:

The sentence cannot be thought about, at least by me: it must be lived. Later, when it is completed, it can be thought about with a certain profit, but no sooner. Sentences, paragraphs, chapters, novels all grow from my imagination in the same fashion: indeed, the sentence is the cell beyond which the life of the book cannot be traced, a novel being a structure of such cells: most must be vital or the body is dead. In another sense, only the sentence exists or at any rate can be proved to exist. Even at the stage of the paragraph things are becoming theoretical and arbitrary. A "novel" is an utter hallucination: no definition of it, for example, can really distinguish it from a laundry list. But a sentence—there you have something essential, to which nothing can be added and from which nothing can be taken. (23 May 1979)

In *Who Is Teddy Villanova?* Berger's fondness for the individual sentence combines with his tendency toward paratactic constructions to produce a tour de force macaronic of prose styles and literary conventions, certainly the most pronounced and sustained example of paratactic style in his novels. Appropriately enough, however, *Nowhere*, the sequel to *Who Is Teddy Villanova?*, in which its protagonist, Russel Wren, encounters a fantastic mythical kingdom with obvious ties to Butler's Erewhon, also exists in paratactic relationship to its antecedent—the only way in which to describe a travel-to-imaginary-lands sequel to a private-eye novel. Moreover, *Nowhere* shifts its focus, from the linguistic parataxis so heavily employed in the dialogue and narrative voice of *Who Is Teddy Villanova?* to the cultural parataxis of social and philosophical codes in Berger's impossible kingdom of Saint Sebastian. Individual sentences are so archly crafted in the former as to strain their credibility in the reader's eyes and ears, while sentences in the latter (with delightful exceptions) are much less noteworthy for their stylistic panache than for their ideational or referential functions. Despite their superficial differences, however, Berger's eighth and thirteenth novels, published eight years apart, are fundamentally linked by the sensibility of their common protagonist, Russel Wren, private investigator.

Who Is Teddy Villanova? invokes all of the formula patterns of the classic American hard-boiled detective novel. But the real mysteries in this novel have nothing to do with traditional down-at-the-heel private eyes. One of its primary mysteries for the reader is how the book's heavy emphasis on literary structure avoids its narrator's suspiciously reflexive-sounding condemnation of decadent contemporary art forms, "occupied solely with structure and not substance." Another mystery for us to try to figure out is why this contemporary American detective story is narrated, in Berger's words, "in a rococo style reminiscent by turns of Thomas De Quincey, Thomas Babington Macaulay, and Sir Thomas Malory."

This novel displays the characteristic diction of the hard-boiled formula, but with a manic inconsistency: the private eye's secretary speaks from the pages of Hammett and Chandler, while her boss, the garrulous Russel Wren, speaks as though quoting Macaulay (as another character pointedly observes). A police detective introduces himself, saying, "I'll show you my identification, if you'll me yours, as Henry James might say," while other detectives self-consciously spout jargon from TV shows. One ostensible villain orders Wren to shut his "fucking flytrap" and elaborates, "Gonna say one thing once and ain't gonna say it again, so get it straight the one time I say it, because you ain't gonna hear it anymore . . . because I ain't gonna chew my cabbage twice" (10). Wren's response to this advice must be a stylistic first for private eyes on any continent or in any literature, as he muses: "Of course . . . if your statement proves unusually complex, there might well be some advantage in repetition, using alternative terms and varying syntaxes, not only for the sake of sheer verbal charm, but also with an eye to the state of affairs in the English language, in which, as one authority asserts, the only exact synonyms are *furze* and *gorse*" (10).

Wren is an ex-instructor of English and Berger has cheerfully added that he regrets not mentioning that Wren is "a constant reader of PMLA though he has left the academy and is trying to go straight" (2 April 1977). Allusion rather than detection is his strength, a twist signaled by the novel's opening line—"Call me Russel Wren." However, Melville's Ishmael would seem to serve as Wren's mentor only insofar as we can easily imagine Wren's skimming over the narrative chapters in *Moby Dick* to get to its scattered expositions on cetology. Denied an Ahab to observe or anything as real as a whale to pursue, Wren is reduced to a series of fish (and fishy) metaphors. Confronted by a thug who is a huge whale of a male, Wren can only notice that he slips through a narrow doorway "as deftly as a perch fins among subaqueous rocks." Describing the aftereffects of a punch by this giant, Wren does his own violence to the tradition of hard-boiled metaphors: "Sam's image registered on my retinas as if I were staring through lenses of lemon-lime Jell-O in which banana rounds were embedded. My neck seemed to support a beer barrel, and my thorax was a construction of pipe cleaners. Only mixed metaphors will serve here: I was a chrestomathy of them at this juncture" (14). When the thug next appears, sprawled on the floor of an elevator that had descended "with its noise so suggestive of the trappings of Marley's ghost, i. e., as if hung with chains and cashboxes," Wren retreats into ever more elaborate description: "If he was not as dead as the cold lasagna on which the tomato sauce has begun to darken, I was a Dutchman. The gaudy and, in the absence of blood, inappropriate metaphor actually came to mind at the moment, as a willed ruse to lure me away from panic—the fundamental purpose of most caprices of language, hence the American wisecrack—but it failed" (21).

If we assume that this passage presents one of the rare instances when Wren's unique sensibility might overlap with that of his creator, it casts *Who Is Teddy Villanova?* in new light, since the novel can perhaps best be described, not as a story, but as an elaborately extended caprice of language. Certainly, the novel's fundamental message is that language is indeed capricious. Wren, who aspires to complete the writing of a play, fails to recognize that the bizarre sequence of events that engulfs him is nothing but a play orchestrated by his landlord to influence the detective to give up his office lease. And more bizarre than the events staged for this purpose is the wordplay they occasion, as even more troubling to Wren than accusations of murder and drug dealing are charges that he is a bogus intellectual. Character after character comments on Wren's dialogue, praising his use and pronunciation of *disparate*, groaning at his seeming resort to mixed metaphor, criticizing his "eighteenth-century billingsgate" in a moment of crisis. For his part, Wren feels most abused, not when struck or duped, but when linguistically outperformed, as by a detective who correctly uses *superfetation*, forcing Wren to admit to himself that he "had never heard that word in speech, and never read it but in the text of T. S. Eliot."

To a writer who has described himself as "essentially a voyeur of copulating words," the play of language is of course an end in itself. Who can doubt that when Berger has Wren say to a police detective, criticizing the employment of the detective's hands as the two men attempt to keep Wren's secretary from falling out of a window, "This wench is my ward. . . . Toy with her fine foot if you like, but eschew her quivering thigh and the demesnes that there adjacent lie" (216), the author is simply putting together words he fancies, in a syntax that pleases him? Indeed, *Who Is Teddy Villanova?* may be most significant for its suggestion that Berger's allegiance to language, to the glories of the individual sentence, is at least as strong as, if not stronger than, his allegiance to the form of the novel.

But Berger's relentless wordplay in *Who Is Teddy Villanova?* may also serve a function with more tangible human implications. When Wren proudly claims, "I think I have demonstrated here that I am nothing but a loyal product of my cultural heritage," his reference is local, explaining his decision to aid in the apprehension of two men alleged to be counterfeiters by a female treasury agent—who herself turns out to be an imposter. In the larger context of Berger's novel, however, Wren's pride should strike the reader as a sad assessment, a clue that his (and our) cultural heritage has been debased precisely by the counterfeits of language.

Unlike the legendary detectives of both British and American traditions, Wren's penchant for precise observation is limited to the inconsequential and is eclipsed only by his passion for precise diction, a trait that imbues the commonplaces of hard-boiled prose with unexpected twists. When struck by an archetypal "ham-fisted" punch, Wren primly observes that his assailant's hand was "the size and consistency of the fleshy side of a loin of pork" (8–9). Such a blow clearly calls for the subsequent Chandleresque "dive into a pool of darkness," but Wren instead notes, "I had no consciousness of my backward velocity," and comes to with the meticulous and incongruously mannered realization: "My loafers were in a position just ahead of his coal-barge brogans, a yard from where I slumped; meanwhile, my feet, twisted on their edges and crushed under the crease between thigh and buttock, were only stockinged: he had knocked me out of my shoes!" (9).

That Wren thinks in ornately clothed clichés is not surprising, since he is almost incapable of thinking in his own terms. His referent base for thought and action consists almost entirely of received ideas. He misperceives *everything* because he perceives only through received expectation patterns—whether those of the formula codes of American and British detective stories, those of mythology, those of racial stereotyping, or those of formula television shows. Indeed, so semiotically voracious is Wren that a single word, particularly if a proper name, can send him in headlong flight after scenarios eagerly inferred from its etymology or connotations.

Although Wren never realizes that this tendency gives rise to most of the problems in his life, other characters frequently tell him as much. Zwingli, the erudite detective whose greatest contempt is reserved, not for the criminal, but for the bogus intellectual, points out to Wren; "I suspect you are living the legend of the private eye, which I confess I had always believed mythical" (98). More accurately, Zwingli might have observed, after the fashion of Lévi-Strauss, that the legend was mythical but the myth was living Wren. As another character observes of Wren's typically stereotyped conception of her occupation as a stewardess: "I don't know whether anybody could live up to your appetite for the legendary, Russel, which applies in all areas of experience. Which is why so many people have found it possible to dupe you so easily" (178). And duped he is, hoaxed at every turn, because he can understand reality only through codes of expectation and behavior that are patently literary and have little or nothing to do with the events of his experience. Wren's life is governed by linguistic and formulaic codes designed to create and advance works of fiction. As he slavishly tries to wrestle his experience into conformity with essentially literary patterns of plot, motivation, and character, these codes "think him"—just as to a great extent we, the readers of his or any story, are guided or "thought" by the traditional codes of the novel. In the case of *Who Is Teddy Villanova?*, however, we are confronted by such a paratactic mélange of these codes that Berger's novel demands our creative involvement as well as our attention.

The greatest appeal of *Who Is Teddy Villanova?*, a novel that exuberantly shows us what's in a name (nothing, everything, a novel!), lies for me exactly in the challenge of making personal sense of its kinds of parataxis. This, perhaps more than any other Berger novel, invites readers to take a step back from their reading, to look over their own shoulders, and to assess their options and obligations as interpreters. No less and no more improbable an authority on detective stories than Gertrude Stein has decreed that the best are those where "nobody is either dead or not dead" and has suggested that the best of all would be "a detective story of how to write."[12] That is as good a description as any of what happens as Russel Wren narrates his misadventures. More important, Wren offers the reader a detective story of *how to read*—the most explicit statement of a concern running throughout Berger's novels.

Nowhere

Precisely to the extent that he proves a disastrous detective, Russel Wren exhibits traits that would make him a successful literary critic: his compulsion to infer motives and to make connections based almost exclusively on philological evidence. In this passion for hypostatized order, Wren joins himself, not to the successful traditions of ratiocination represented by Poe's Dupin and Doyle's Holmes, but to the self-destructive tradition of "reckless discernment" made infamous by Erik Lonnrot, the detective protagonist of Jorge Luis Borges's "Death and the Compass." While extended comparison with that Borges story would undoubtedly bring new light to a reading of *Who Is Teddy Villanova?*, I mention it more for what it suggests for our understanding of *Nowhere*, a novel that transplants Russel Wren's misadventures from the legendary setting of Manhattan to the mythical kingdom of Saint Sebastian. For, if *Nowhere* openly acknowledges a part of its ancestry in Samuel Butler's *Erewhon*, it implicitly reveals a greater number of ties to the more abstract, nonideological worlds of Borges and Nabokov. Moreover, as was also true of *Who Is Teddy Villanova?*, this novel argues that for one such as Russel Wren, there can be no world more impossible than that of New York City, no imaginary setting to rival its variety, contradictions, and humiliations.

"Obviously if you've survived in New York City," Wren is told in *Nowhere* by the agent who impresses him into covert service, "you know how to lie and cheat and dissemble: spying should be just your meat" (30). While *Teddy Villanova*'s plot boils down to a city story of the most banal sort—a landlord's machinations to get a tenant to drop a lease—the novel does not, after the manner of the hard-boiled detective story, expose the corrupt underbelly of a big city. Instead, it inventories New York City's *reputed* idiosyncrasies, ironies, and cynicisms. Russel Wren, it must be remembered, is a master only of the received idea, and although he is an inhabitant of Manhattan, his comments about it are exactly what we expect, the familiar litany of city complaints.

Indeed, it can be argued that when Wren is shanghaied ("New-Yorked" might be a more appropriate term today) by a CIA-like government entity to the hitherto unknown (at least to Wren) central European kingdom of Saint Sebastian, the move is actually from a legendary setting to an experiential

one: he is as devoid of received ideas about life in Saint Sebastian as he is sur-
feited with those about life in New York. Moreover, while in Saint Sebastian,
he contrasts its customs, not with those of his native land, but with received
truths about his city.

Its action beginning with what seems to be a terrorist bombing, followed
by the disclosure of a secret government agency that is monitoring the terror-
ists, *Nowhere* opens like so many novels of international intrigue, a point explicitly made by the purported agent of the "Firm," "Bunch," "Troop,"
"Pack," or "Gang," who informs Wren he would better understand what was
going on "if you read any blockbusting thrillers." Although Wren's narrative
occasionally gives a nod to this flimsy frame of the spy thriller, it soon starts
nodding more in the direction of the novel of utopian/dystopian satire, with
an occasional wink at the conventions of dream psychology (Wren grouses
that in America "a grasp of basic Freudianism was now enjoyed by millhand
and shopgirl"). Once again, to describe the form of this Berger novel as anything but paratactic would be to ignore its singular permutations of conventions associated with a wide range of literary traditions. The difference this
time is that Berger's paratactic structure introduces us to a fictional land that
is itself paratactically organized, its codes and institutions manically at odds
with each other.

That Russel Wren would travel to a marvelous kingdom resembling nothing quite so much as those made famous in American movie musicals of the
thirties (or, more accurately still, the *sets* for those musicals, since Saint
Sebastian's colorful open-air markets are made of plastic) is quite in keeping
with his "appetite for the legendary." That modifying forms of the kingdom's
name would sound suspiciously like that of a well-known vineyard in
Sonoma County, California, also reminds us of Wren's keen awareness of
brand names, even in the midst of most amazing events. Indeed, several aspects of life in Saint Sebastian, such as the central importance of its blonds
and the nature of its national encyclopedia, are direct dream-logic extensions
of Wren's thinking in *Teddy Villanova*. But what the reader learns of customs
in Saint Sebastian probably reveals more of Berger's sensibility than of
Wren's, suggesting that even a world based largely on Nietzschean suppositions would be little improvement, the ills of ressentiment beyond even imaginary cure.

Although superficial affinities between *Nowhere* and Samuel Butler's
Erewhon abound, Berger's iconoclasm proves more relentless than Butler's,
extending even to the notion that a satiric society can serve as a criticism of our
own. Indeed, beyond inverting and thus invoking Butler's title, Berger's title
exists as the only answer to the friendly prostitute who says to Wren: "I don't

know, Rus, sometimes I think it oughta be better than this. But then I think, *Where?*" (189).

Curiously enough, Berger's comments about the writing of this novel rarely mention Butler, citing instead More's *Utopia* and Eliot's *Idea of a Christian Society* as his novel's precursors. While working on an early version of *Nowhere*, he also declared his intent to "promote all my social ideas, one of which is that in the perfect society there is no legal freedom whatever, virtually everything being against the law—but no law is ever enforced" (24 February 1978).

Saint Sebastian's most radical feature is surely that it acknowledges the insolubility of human problems. Its Ministry of Clams exists solely for the purpose of accepting denunciations for unanswerable complaints and insoluble problems, dutifully filing, then forgetting, all complaints. Puzzled when asked if that process actually satisfies complainants, the ministry's receptionist patiently explains to Wren that human beings can never be satisfied, supporting her claim by asking if he knew of "any social problem that was truly solved" (141). Wren, who earlier in his narrative has acerbically mentioned passing in New York City a sign marking the future site of "some state agency working for the abolition of envy," feebly protests this view, but Berger, his creator, embraces it, implicitly offering his novels more as agents of the Ministry of Clams than of social or psychological change or reform. In 1975 Berger outlined this belief in a letter to his friend Zulfikar Ghose: "When I met [Arthur Koestler]—after he said something favorable about *Killing Time*—he said he could not help trying to 'save the world.' He said this wryly, of course, and then asked me whether I felt the same urge. I said no, that I wouldn't walk across the street to save the world, because I did not see it as a problem to which there was a solution."[13]

Accordingly, the kingdom of Saint Sebastian offers in its unique approach to social custom neither examples that reveal the error in our conflicting approaches nor examples so wrongheaded as to obliquely point the way to improving our own social practice—a stance made clear by the fact that for better or worse those customs are overthrown within the novel by revolution. Instead, what *Nowhere* offers us is a series of intriguing propositions, some appealing, some reprehensible, all delightful in their quirkiness. Berger would seem to be in complete agreement with the character who tells Wren that her "job is to be a stewardess, and not to deal in social theoretics"—as, at bottom, is Wren himself, whose most profound insight into the complicated Sebastiani revolution is simply that "the people who know how to handle themselves seem to be similar, irrespective of ideology" (179).

Just as Erewhon has its College of Unreason, Musical Banks, and Hospital for Incurable Bores, Saint Sebastian presents to Wren its ministries of irony, hoaxes, and disaffection, its economy driven by the "God-given right to be owed money by others," its one scholarly project—the arbitrary and capricious *Encyclopaedia Sebastiana*—and its house for sequestering all authors, Saint Sebastian's most unscrupulous people, from the public. This is a country so inverted as to give tourists constipation, a place, like Erewhon, where the injured party is the defendant before the law and, also like Erewhon, where light hair identifies one for special treatment. Some measure of the difference between Berger's and Butler's mythical kingdoms, however, can be inferred from the uniquely Bergeresque twist that in Saint Sebastian, blond hair condemns one to inferior status; since all are born blond, only "moral weaklings" refuse to dye their hair a darker color.

Neither an ideal society nor a dystopian horror, Saint Sebastian is an interesting place structured largely around incorrect received ideas drawn from old American B movies of the thirties and forties. Compulsory attendance at these films, left behind by USO and army personnel after World War II, has supplanted both church and school, now dismissed by a projectionist priest as "poor imitations of life." The real thing, he proudly informs Wren, are old American films. "The virtuous are shown to succeed, the evildoers invariably come to grief, and the general philosophy that informs every picture is that there is a common good, which is recognized by everyone—including the wicked, who of course are opposed to it, but they *know what it is*" (150). Berger's joke is a fantastic society based precisely on the received truths that are supposed to guide our own, a supposition, of course, itself a received truth quite at odds with reality.

In like fashion, we must try to follow, through the convolutions of Berger's irony, Russel Wren's commendably hopeless credo when he tries to counter the charge that humanistic platitudes have no meaning in the real world. "I just wish people would be quietly nice and fair to one another and there would never be any riots, revolutions, wars. I am aware that hope is weak-minded, but I am confident that it is normal amongst the rank and file of all nations, creeds, and breeds" (109). In the context of Wren's character and in the context of *Nowhere*'s semblance, these words reveal a sappy idealism that can only lead to disappointment and worse. I believe they also may mark the precise spot in this novel where Wren's outlook and that of his creator are at one.

Chapter Six

Kickers and Kickees:
Being Invisible, Sneaky People, The Feud, Neighbors, and *The Houseguest*

I have at last found another of the sadomasochistic situations in which, I think, my peculiar strength lies. The suspense comes in trying to identify who's the kicker and who the kickee, *sub specie aeternitatis* or even only in terms of the local supermarket. I always know when I've got the right theme because then I am eager to see what happens each day. With the wrong one I must invent what happens, and that is wearisome and boring for me. One of Groucho Marx's celebrated bon mots was, in rejecting an invitation to join the Lambs Club, "I wouldn't want to belong to a club that would have me as a member." Similarly, I don't like books that I must write!

—Thomas Berger, discussing *Neighbors*, 2 October 1978

Reviews of *Being Invisible,* Thomas Berger's fourteenth novel, refer to its "mocking tone," its "stridency and underlying anger," its "paranoia," or its author's "almost Jacobean feeling for revenge" and his "unforgiving view"—all words and phrases commensurate with Berger's fascination with issues of discriminating "kickers" from "kickees," victims from victimizers.[1] Francine Prose concludes her *New York Times Book Review* piece on the novel by expressing her admiration for precisely these qualities: "As our Government works to persuade us that life is good, that everything is all right, it's an enormous *relief* to hear Mr. Berger's voice: sneering, shrill, combative, insisting that life *isn't* all right or likely to be, that strangers will just as soon kill you as give you the time of day. It is a sign of the times that we feel such affection for Thomas Berger's dogged, cranky courage, and for the denizens of his unwelcoming and chaotic corner of the fictional world."[2]

Readers who find Berger's novels "mocking," "strident," or "unforgiving" mistake his consistent *refusal to be sentimental* with the assertion of patently sentimental criticizing attitudes, but there is an unmistakable hard edge to his writing that does often seem born of cynicism. Indeed, Berger avows, "My point of view when I am being a mere person is altogether cynical," but he adds a crucial clarification: "I rise above myself when in the service of my high office" (8 September 1987). And this distinction is what is missing from the otherwise insightful comment by Francine Prose: the cynicism possibly attributable to Berger the implied author should not be confused with the worldview of his novels, nor with our experience in reading them. The last thing Berger wants is an audience primed to smirk along with the author at the predictable weaknesses of humanity, and his novels never support the familiar alliance between writer and reader as "kickers" against the "kickee" of human nature—understood as the foibles of others.

Berger the "mere person" is hardly unique in his cynicism, or, more properly, that cynicism lies beyond the analysis of the critic and can be inferred only to the extent that Berger identifies himself as standing somewhere in the massive ranks of contemporary and historical cynics. Berger the novelist, however, is a different story. When in the service of that "high office," he consistently rejects cynicism as too simple a point of view—the equally unrigorous inverse of sentimentalism. What may or may not be cynicism in the views of Berger the man becomes inexorably transformed in the dialectical irony of Berger the novelist, whose commitment to try to show "how things *are* as opposed to what they are generally thought to be" brings his scrutiny to bear on the received platitudes of cynicism just as surely as it does on those of meliorism. And when Berger suggests, "I am, in fact, so ironic that often I pursue the inquiry until it turns back and reveals that which has been exposed as illusion or delusion is actually true,"[3] he offers us a particularly useful key to understanding five of his most pointedly ironic novels: *Being Invisible, Sneaky People, The Feud, Neighbors,* and *The Houseguest.* Each of these novels explores, in quite different ways, one of the favorite subjects of Berger's irony, the question "who's the kicker and who the kickee," an exploration of the complicated dynamic of power.

Being Invisible

H. G. Wells writes in *The Invisible Man* that "It is so much easier not to believe in an invisible man." Thomas Berger comments about Wells's work:

One of my all-time favorite themes is Invisibility, and as recently as last week I was trying to begin a novel about a person who had acquired a means of becoming invisible. I wasn't able to get the hang of it for a novel, at least not at this time, but maybe something will come of it in the future. Meanwhile I'm trying something else as outlandish. Wells's *The Invisible Man* is among the few books I have read more than twice. (I also admire my friend Ralph Ellison's novel of almost the same title [omitting the article], but that is an unseen horse of a different color.) (2 March 1983)

Notwithstanding his praise for Wells and Ellison, Berger's contribution to the literature of invisibility may actually have more in common with the visually striking situation posited in Kafka's *Metamorphosis*. A crucial key to understanding Kafka's story is the simple question, What happens if Gregor Samsa awakes one morning to discover that he has *not* been transformed into a giant vermin? In much the same way, the question that should be asked about Fred Wagner, protagonist of *Being Invisible*, Berger's fourteenth novel, is, What happens if Fred does *not* discover that he can will himself to become invisible?

Parallels between the two works are immediate and obvious: just as Gregor gradually realizes his humanity precisely through his "bugness," Fred becomes morally visible only through his experiences with physical invisibility. What both characters most desperately need is nourishment, a matter of the spirit rather than of the flesh, an enigmatic phenomenon whose scarcity is a constant concern throughout Berger's writing. But while Berger's truths are essentially those of Kafka, the world of his fiction runs according to more complicated rules, and Fred Wagner's metamorphosis proves much less costly and much more humorous than Gregor's. Along the way, Berger's novel, while addressing the salient issues of the invisibility formula as codified in both film and literature, provides a wry investigation of the petty tyrannies of quotidian life, suggesting that before the onslaught of banality, even invisibility proves powerless.

Most generously praised as "not the only person never to have discovered a principle as far-reaching in its consequences as the lever," Fred Wagner, a disappointed novelist (seventeen pages in six and a half years), failed husband, demeaned brother, and generally humiliated human being, writes copy for novelty items sold in mail-order catalogs. His genuine sensitivity to language and his modest gift for verbal precision are exhausted in writing ads for a combination ballpoint pen and flashlight or a cylindrical transistor radio that fits inside a toiletpaper roll, and Fred's surface complacency gloves all manner of deeply seated resentments. Although a competent "good soldier," he has been passed over for promotion at work and is soon to be fired; his wife has left him ("He assumed he loved her to some degree, and he knew he hated her for leaving him"); his acquaintances seem to treat him with indifference, if not contempt; and his own self-esteem has crumbled. "He sometimes wondered whether he was not a unit but rather a collection of disparate parts which, finding themselves thrown together, made the best of what easily could have been seen as an unfortunate accident" (5).

A chrestomathic index to petty humiliations, Fred "was the sort of man who could lose face by the return of a letter with postage-due charges," just as he can feel embarrassed when forced to make an ungrammatical response to the greeting of a doorman. Indeed, "losing face" may have been the figurative first step in Fred's literal discovery that he could will himself to become invisible, the ultimate stage in the disintegration of self-image. Yet Fred's fantastic ability does not confer fantastic power: when invisible, he remains a disappointed novelist, his wife has still left him, and the world, which barely noticed him in the first place, now sees him not at all. Since it does preclude an audience, invisibility can restrict the scope of public embarrassment, but it does nothing to assuage Fred's ravenous private guilt, as he is "so sensitive to humiliation as to feel it vicariously when he himself was but an observer of an experience in which it was no more than an impending possibility" (12). An artist only in his ability to appropriate guilt, Fred, on invisibly observing someone rifling through his office desk, feels not anger but "humiliation that the man would not encounter anything valuable enough to steal" (78).

Indeed, Berger relentlessly subjects his protagonist to the exquisite gamut of petty humiliations possible in post offices, restaurants, public restrooms, doctors' offices, and elevators—recasting these spaces as the banal torture chambers of modern life. What emerges from Fred's misadventures in these arenas is Berger's sense that victimization by a surly postal clerk or arrogant waiter proves no less instructive of the dynamics of power than do the more dramatic examples of physical or psychological abuse. In the world of Berger's fiction, small indignities debilitate even more inexorably than do large injustices; whereas the latter are sometimes subject to redress, the former usually are not. Fred himself announces what could be an initial assumption of all Berger's fiction: "the shift of power is always a fascinating process" (174). And just as "through being invisible Wagner learned many truths that otherwise would have been inaccessible" (3), Berger's readers soon realize the pervasive power of the unreasonable in invisible life, just as in visible life.

Or, to put it another way, many truths continue to elude Fred despite his invisibility. Foremost among these are the recurring patterns of his uniformly disastrous relationships with women. Left by a wife he clearly misunderstood (as indeed he misunderstands almost everyone), Fred becomes the almost helpless sexual partner, in rapid succession, for two women who make no effort whatsoever to understand him, opportunistically "seeing" him only as a blank surface for the inscription of their own wills. A madcap series of seductions by a neighbor, a seemingly archetypal lusty widow, and by an equally archetypal-seeming innocent young coworker (both of whom defy Fred's expectations) dispels his conviction that after his wife he would never attract another woman, but it intensifies his fear that he lacks "existential substance." "If he fell in a remote forest with no one about to hear the crash, would there be one" (200). Invisibility, arguably Fred's only intriguing feature, plays no role in the designs of either woman. Indeed, his invisibility can only be a redundancy to them, since both already look *through* him, his desires and interests being totally irrelevant to their respective purposes.

The neighbor, Sandra Eng, and the coworker, Mary Alice Phillips, like so many of Berger's women characters, prove to be consummate artists of the real rather than of the merely representational, as they consistently remap the terrain of their situations, manipulating Fred to every possible advantage. Compared with the smothering, robust vitality of Sandra, the calculating petulance of Mary Alice, and even his wife's quiet, single-minded determination to carve out business success in the art world, Fred's life seems to have no core, being organized only around diffuse resentment. In the company of these women, Fred \ *should* be invisible, his uncertain substance totally eclipsed by the bright flames of their respective wills.

The creative faculties that fail Fred as a novelist also fail him as an invisible man, and he initially thinks of his ability only as "a device to avoid inconvenience or embarrassment, not as a means for the shirking of responsibility" (54). He first employs his invisibility to secure a single postage stamp, intending to pay for it while circumventing the indifference of postal clerks. Even that limited objective eludes him as he drops more coins than the stamp is worth, actually losing money in the transaction. He next uses his power in order to delay a pest of a coworker from boarding an elevator, resorts to it to avoid the embarrassment of not having enough money with him to pay a lunch-counter check, then invisibly snatches a cigarette from another coworker's hand, thus punishing her for the effrontery of eating and smoking at the same time. After invisibly delivering a kick to the rear of one of his antagonists (a slapstick gesture firmly codified both in Wells's novel and in Universal's Invisible Man films), Fred finally applies his newfound ability to robbing a bank, only to return the money as soon as he realizes that the young, female bank teller from whose drawer he has taken it would undoubtedly be blamed for its disappearance. As is true of almost all Berger's protagonists before him, Fred remains the captive of a relentless awareness of responsibility: "Thus despite his extraordinary gift, Wagner was still as much at the mercy of events as he ever was. Perhaps he lacked the basic stuff to be a legendary invisible personage, one of the pioneering titans of the tradition, on whose shoulders all future unseen practitioners would stand. Perhaps he was a poetaster, not a poet, of invisibility, his experiences a mere doggerel of the ability to elude the eye" (221).

More properly, Fred's failures assure him and Berger's readers of the first real education in the arcane matters of invisibility. Ever the scrupulous prober of the traditions he celebrates, Berger takes pains to specify that *his* invisible personage extends his invisibility to all he touches, as long as he maintains contact with the object or person. By this means, Fred is delivered from the invisibility formula's well-codified meteorological limitations: invisible only when completely naked, traditional invisible men and women not only have been singularly uncomfortable when practicing their métier in the winter or inclement weather but would also be undone when rain or snow revealed their outlines, establishing their presences through the very absence of that which they displaced. His practical discoveries, such as of the difficulty of negotiating stairs when he can't see his feet or of related problems in using a urinal, parallel those made by Griffin, Wells's invisible man, but in his philosophical realization that invisibility is ill-suited for solving social problems, Fred becomes the first in the distinguished line of literary invisible personages to explore rigorously the implications of his condition. For example, he admits to himself that his newfound ability would not count for much in his wife's practical aesthetic, since it could not be appreciated for its style or evaluated: "To Babe that would be a trick, not a talent; an ingenious trick to be sure, but if *he* could have learned how to do it, so could others. Whereas talent was unique" (241). Indeed, discovering that being invisible has no effect on the "fundamental way the world worked," the previously unnoticed Fred now finds it impossible to get people to notice his invisibility: "In all the world there was no one who would willingly and with more than a polite interest serve as his audience " (248).

Once Fred arrives at this conclusion, he decides to make a legal and domestic separate peace by faking suicide through drowning. While unsure of the particulars of starting over, he sees in the appearance of suicide the one bold stroke capable of resolving the various entanglements of his life. When, however, he sees that the approaching young woman he hopes will witness his plunge into the river is being mugged, he invisibly subdues her armed assailant. As Berger's unobtrusive but occasionally philosophical narrator has earlier deadpanned, "having the ability to vanish does, sooner or later, work a change in a person" (93). For the first time in the novel, if not in his life, Fred feels a kind of spiritual nourishment in truly looking after someone who not only acknowledges, but is obviously impressed by, his efforts, only to learn that the young woman, Catherine Rider, is getting married next week and that she wants Fred to meet her fiancé.

Berger's dirtiest trick on Fred proves transitory, however, as the meeting with the couple occasions an argument when Catherine's effete fiancé reveals he is too fearful of possible retribution to press charges against her psychopathic assailant. Having to choose between Fred's promise that he can defend her from all harm and her fiancé's warning that the only way to deal with a homicidal maniac is to stay out of his way, Catherine utters the one phrase capable of changing Fred's life, "I believe in Fred." For once, someone believes in his essence, after which the belief in his invisibility becomes a mere footnote.

A unique focus on de-emphasizing the import of invisibility, however, should not be confused with singular concern, as Berger's novel also offers readers a characteristically Bergeresque running commentary on language use, as well as an ironic framing of alternatives to Berger's creative aesthetic. The former concern emerges from a series of superficial verbal run-ins that establish Fred's painstaking linguistic competence but also usually indict his rhetorical judgment, revealing his faulty sense of proportion. For example, Fred who has just been fired, tells one of his recent colleagues, "It's been nice working with you." She corrects him, "We just worked at the same place, not really with one another." He then spitefully notes that "when speaking of only two persons, preferred usage calls for 'each other,' not 'one another,' which is reserved for three or more"—only to be himself chastised for a construction suggesting that "Preferred Usage is doing the speaking" (168). Objecting to an art gallery owner's use of the word *sculpt*, Fred specifies: "'Sculpture.'. . . The verb is 'to sculpture.' There is no such word as 'sculpt.'" "Why, sure there is," his antagonist enthusiastically replies. "I use it all the time" (236).

By far the more interesting and significant subtext appears in the novel's opposition of Fred's failed aesthetic to the apparently false aesthetic of his nemesis, Siv Zirko, an egomaniacal sculptor whose business interests are now managed by Fred's estranged wife. In every way Fred's antithesis, Zirko is so self-centered that the world itself is rendered invisible to him beyond the glare of his immediate desires. Zirko's art consists of separated reproductions of his body parts—hand, eyes, nose, penis—right down to clear plastic bubbles purporting to display "ARTIST'S SHIT, PISS, SWEAT, SPIT, AND COME" (91). Moreover, Zirko's announced aesthetic both implicitly mocks Fred's predicament of moral invisibility and presents a rationale clearly at odds with Berger's own creative sensibility:

"Like most people," Zirko says, "I never before actually ever looked at myself. I mean *really* looked. Or maybe I looked without seeing. And what is art anyway but a way of seeing? And if you think about it, where should an artist begin if not with himself? This is especially true with a sculptor, to which is added the truth that can be learned through tactility. So I have dissected myself. I have let you in on my secrets. Use them well. Touch me, stroke me, fondle me, caress me. Let's exchange love!" (90)

While Berger makes fun of Zirko's aesthetic, he also presents the artist's insufferable ego as a truly powerful phenomenon, an odious but irrepressible natural force. Thrown out of the window of his third-floor loft by an enraged and invisible Fred, Zirko escapes death by falling into an open truckful of discarded mattresses—only to remap the incredible sequence of events as the start of a new style in his art. Zirko is crude, self-centered, unreflective, and callous—precisely the qualities, it would seem, necessary for success as an artist in the world of Berger's novel. While Siv's art may be patently bogus (Fred concludes that "the shit encased in plastic was not art, but shit"), his vitality makes him a perversely appealing character, yet another in the long line of Berger's outrageous rogues who finally seem to display a kind of integrity in their consistent excesses.

Zirko's grandiose art of the self contrasts with the paralyzing self-effacement of Fred's view of his own art, the novel in which he tried to shape an autobiographical account of his mother's illness and death: "What was wrong with this for purposes of fiction was that it had already taken place in time: to write about it was either to be a reporter or a liar, in either of which roles he would have felt as though he were corrupting private histories" (150).

Ostensibly opposites in every imaginable respect, Fred and Zirko ironically unite in their shared assumption that art is essentially mimetic, a function of reality rather than of the creative imagination. Finally, Fred and Zirko represent opposite sides of the same coin. Fred has no talent for putting himself "inside suppositious skins" to "feel the heartbeats of fancy as if they represented the circulation of his own blood"; Zirko, of course, could never conceive even the possibility of such a displacement. That Berger's fancy frames these aesthetics in seeming opposition to each other and in real opposition to his own illustrates the characteristic complexity of his ironizing.

Being Invisible offers yet another twist to Berger's investigation of the nature of kickers and kickees. The novel's wry and rueful humor suggests that "under the aspect of eternity," invisibility may bend our understanding of reality, but changes little of the working of human nature. And Berger's final irony is that the basic structure of his novel implicates us, his readers, in the very vagaries of human nature we pride ourselves in identifying (kicking) in the lives of his characters. Just as surely as Siv Zirko's robust solipsism seems set up within the semblance of the novel for criticism, if not ridicule, Berger's work seduces readers into a similarly solipsistic empathy for, or identification with, Fred Wagner's marginal plight. For, whatever his failings, Fred *is never* invisible to us, as he is always center stage, frozen in the spotlight of Berger's narrative scheme. Fred may be a marginal character in his fictional world, but he always remains the main character in our reading.

Fred's prominence in the narrative almost insures that we will sentimentalize our response, the narrator's point of view ever directing our attention toward Fred's invisibility and away from the clear evidence that others are as invisible to Fred as he is to them. His story can be seen, in one sense, in terms of a sequence of characters initially as overlooked or misperceived by him as he is by them, and the action of the novel consists largely, not of his exploits, but of their forcing themselves into his sight. As these characters come into better focus for Fred, they also come into better focus for Berger's readers, presenting the nagging prospect that they may turn out to be more interesting than Fred, even if he is Berger's protagonist. Through this subtle process, Berger demonstrates a way in which the reader as kicker can become reader as kickee, victimized by expectations just as surely as are Berger's characters.

Social or moral invisibility, after all, is a mass rather than individual threat, and the phenomenon inheres within the conventions of the novel just as surely as it does within the conventions of society. It is to this final irony that Berger's title directs our attention—to the universal processes of invisibility, rather than to the sentimental uniqueness of a single invisible man. Explaining one of Fred's many surprises, Berger's narrator philosophizes that "whatever the milieu, at any given time someone must always be the most newly arrived" (223). In the milieu of Berger's fiction, the most newly arrived, of course, is always the reader.

Sneaky People

Sneaky People is Berger's seventh and, with the possible exception of *Reinhart's Women,* his gentlest novel, notwithstanding the fact that much of its action concerns plans for a murder. The novel chronicles the coming of a age of a fifteen-year-old boy, Ralph Sandifer, in a dreamy small-town world where nothing is nearly as bucolic as it seems and all situations are heavily ironic. Given the scheme of Berger's novels as "celebrations" of classic genres, *Sneaky People* almost has to be a tribute to Booth Tarkington's *Penrod* or *Seventeen.* But this is a story of several different kinds of initiations, and its focus is divided among five adult characters in addition to Ralph. Ralph's father, Buddy, owns a used-car lot and plans to have one of his employees murder Ralph's mother. Naomi, the drab, mousy-seeming mother, secretly writes and sells pornography, trading on her knowledge that "because sexual congress was ludicrous in life, its depiction must necessarily follow suit, nay, go it more than one better if interest were to be provoked from the reader, who having come into the world with genitals was himself a born clown" (279). Contrasted with Naomi's imagination of preposterous sex is the considerable experience of Laverne, Buddy's mistress, a good-natured sometime whore and full-time pragmatist. Another of Buddy's employees, Leo Kirsch, knows women only through his long-suffering submission to a domineering and hypochondriac mother ("You missed it, Leo. . . . You missed my hemorrhage") and through his fantasy letters to young girls pictured in the newspaper. In fact, *Sneaky People* presents quite a catalog of possible male-female relationships, almost all of which are primarily structured by misunderstanding— both of the self and of others. Consequently, most of the humor of the novel arises from situations that deflate the hypostatized rhetorical worlds that each character has come up with to make sense of, or to mask, the reality of his or her life. Finally, Berger's characters are "sneaky" simply because they are human, and their secrets are nothing more or less than the inherent condition of their existence. As D. Keith Mano so aptly noted in his review of *Sneaky People*, Berger "prefers the padded bra in all of us."[4]

Apart from the humor of its situations, this book creates a steady background of genial vernacular banter, a world of familiar but now-neglected colloquial commonplaces, exclamations, and retorts. As much as, or more than, even *Little Big Man,* this book reveals that Berger should be acclaimed for his ear as well as his vision. He has described *Sneaky People* as his "tribute to the American language of 1939—to be philologically precise, that of the lower-middle class in the eastern Middle West, on which I am an authority as on nothing else." Characteristically, Berger concluded his description of this celebration of language by saying, "I can think of no pretext more serious, morally or aesthetically, for the writing of a novel."[5] He explains: "American English had its great flowering in the 1920s and 30s, lay dormant during World War II except in the military forces—he who has never been under arms *never* learns authentically to curse—and has degenerated badly since the advent of the television news broadcast, in which speech has become the sniveling lackey to impulses of light. . . . The possibilities for wit—and thus for life—decline with the language."[6]

Certainly, the language of *Sneaky People* is anything *but* homogenized and is the source of the great majority of the book's wit and energy. Ralph's mother, for example, strikes even her son as speaking a bit oddly ("almost English, sometimes reminding him of Merle Oberon"), and her writing style under the name Mary Joy is even more noteworthy, as in the following: "New Year's Day, 8 A.M.—Lying here upon my pink satin sheets, my black-lace nightie drawn up above the twin swellings of my creamy-white breasts, tipped with erect rubicund nipples surrounded by large roseate aureolae, I greet the fresh new year with an exploratory finger in the deepest recess of the warm, moist grotto between my heaving ivory thighs, and think of another Jan. 1 on which, like the year, I was too a virgin" (252–53).

Berger's narration in this novel subtly approaches tour de force in its combination of vernacular diction and rhythm with serpentine syntax, as sentence after sentence winds toward increasingly specific images. When Ralph hears a friend revile the woman he has just become infatuated with, his reaction is described in typically humorous specificity:

That Hauser referred to Laverne Linda Lorraine; that drunkenly they had been heading for her staircase on Saturday night; that his kind friend on the one hand was on the other a stinking, vile, obscene criminal whose filthy tongue should be ripped out—all this was clear.

But it could also be regarded as an established truth that, except in movies and ancient narratives such as the series about Frank Merriwell, a normal modern individual did not commit violence in response to verbal attacks on a woman's honor, especially those made in ignorance by an imbecile who no doubt had been home all afternoon playing with himself while perusing the little eight-page fuckbook the edges of which could be seen protruding from his back pocket as he climbed the steps. (178)

Sentences such as these are the norm in *Sneaky People,* supplying a kind of syntactic joy all their own, in addition to giving us humorous insights into the thinking of Berger's characters.

The Feud

Berger's twelfth novel, *The Feud,* written some seven years after the publication of *Sneaky People,* resurrects both the mid-thirties small-town semblance of the earlier work and its fascination with the spoken language of that time. "*The Feud* is my most modest work," Berger has written, " a little memoir of the place and time of my youth, more or less the same *mise en scene* as that of *Sneaky People,* but the characters are of a lower class" (7 Dec 1982). In another note, the author indicated that he thought of *The Feud* "as a kind of

Dreiserian slice of life" (25 April 1982). Berger's descriptions are accurate to a point, but this "most modest work" was judged best novel of 1984 by the judges' panel for the Pulitizer Prize (a decision administratively overruled in favor of William Kennedy's *Ironweed*).[7] A paragon of prose efficiency even in Berger's exquisitely precise canon, *The Feud* posits a richly textured semblance with a perfectly controlled minimum of exposition and limns its features in record time. Almost devoid of time-marking brand-name identifications, Berger's narration is at once generic and precise, as when specifying that a rake "was not the implement made specifically for leaves, but rather the iron-spiked rake used to scratch the ground for gardening." The most extended physical description in the novel is of a basement, and from the fondly detailed precision of a few masterful passages such as this grows the power of Berger's fictional world:

Stacks of newspapers and magazines, neatly tied, sat on the concrete floor near the bottom of the steps, no doubt awaiting collection by the Boy Scouts. There was a toilet in the Bullard basement, with a crude door of wood slats, wide open at the moment: the seat was in the raised position and looked split. Beyond this were the stationary washtubs of soapy-textured galvanized metal, and then one entire corner was filled with a workbench and its attendant tools, the smaller ones hung neatly on wall hooks and the largest, a wood-turning lathe, mounted at one end of the long bench top. Toward the other extremity was a vise of the under-table type. Everything was very clean, but it looked as if it had seen use enough: the blades of the edged tools had that subdued sheen of veteran steel, and the wooden handles were darkened and polished with the natural oils of the hand. (44–45)

Moreover, this novel's apparent Dreiserian simplicity masks one of Berger's most sophisticated narrative voices, one with a point of view at once Olympian and warmly understanding of the fourteen characters whose sensibilities it so clearly establishes. At times historically omniscient ("Jack suspected he had made a mistake that day in the garage, and he still regretted it, as men do, many years later, though by then he was filing dispatches from the other side of the world"), this narrative voice smoothly segues in and out of the more limited points of view of selected characters, as in describing a boy's thoughts in a moment of ardor: "She had a sweet, damp smell, like the bathtub after it had been used by his sister, who had left home by now and worked in the city as a cashier in a moviehouse, and therefore he hadn't smelled that in a while: it was not perfume as such" (31). From the wide range of its narrative stances, and particularly from the restrained wisdom of its disembodied narrator, Berger's novel derives a quiet, timeless authority. Most important, however, *The Feud* presents not a slice of life so much as a model of a thoroughly contingent world, one much more consonant with the propositions of systems theory than with the morally pegged determinism of Dreiser.

Berger may set *The Feud* in a small town of the thirties, but his fictional world operates according to systematic principles not scientifically codified before the 1960s and 1970s and—due to their starkly unsentimental rigor—still not aesthetically codified in fiction. For example, in place of Dreiser's selectively punitive determinism, Berger presents a world uniformly described in terms of consequences rather than intentions. In the world of *The Feud* almost anything may happen, and everything that does occur impinges upon everything else: change any aspect of the system, and all aspects will be affected. Try to refinish an old piece of furniture, and you start a feud; start a feud, and your family ricochets off its events in wildly new directions. Chaotic in normative or moral terms, such a fictional world is simply an unexpectedly realistic model of our "real" world when understood in terms of systems mechanics. Of course, the important point here is, not that Berger understands or could possibly care about systems theory, but that it offers a clear explanation for the way he presents life in his fiction. And once again we discover that the conventional-seeming surface of Berger's celebration of a novel form (this time the Dreiserian slice of life) masks a radical substructure that is uniquely Berger's.

In its most narrow sense, Berger's title refers to the sudden eruption and three-day playing out of an intense feud between the family of Dolf Beeler, a resident of Hornbeck, and the family of Bud Bullard, who lives in neighboring Millville. Fueled by misunderstanding, misplaced pride, pathological insecurity, small-town xenophobia, self-serving interpretations of events, and the convergence of an incredible sequence of coincidences, this feud is finally remarkable for nothing quite so much as its representation of the *way things actually happen* in life—a sign of its realism rather than of its adherence to realistic literary conventions. The action of this novel and the thoughts of its characters quickly reveal that the dynamics of feuding, quaint though the term may sound, is one of the received structures of human experience, a mold just waiting to be filled—whether by Montagues and Capulets, Hatfields and McCoys, or Beelers and Bullards. *Inimicare humanun est* (to feud is human).

What's more, this received structure isolates Berger's fascination with discerning kickers and kickees, in a reciprocal system guaranteeing that those labels will alternate as the feud progresses. In many ways, feuding is the perfect dynamic for all of Berger's primary concerns, as not only do feuds posit a process in which kickers and kickees—victims and victimizers—are continuously being redefined but the feuds are themselves also inevitably structured by language and inevitably question our understanding of freedom. Small wonder that many of Berger's most perceptive readers judge *The Feud* his most perfectly crafted novel.

When middle-aged plant foreman Dolf Beeler decides to make good on a longstanding promise to his wife to refinish an old piece of furniture, he goes to Bud Bullard's hardware store in the adjoining small town to buy the necessary paint remover. Told by Bullard's son that he must throw away his cigar, Dolf replies that it is not lit, occasioning a rapidly escalating series of conflicts that culminates in Bullard's cousin Reverton pulling a gun on Dolf, handcuffing him, and forcing him to kneel on the floor and apologize. Freed moments later, Dolf remains mentally paralyzed: "He could not understand what had happened to him, how on a normal Saturday morning he could have had such a terrible experience" (7). Dolf can't, but readers soon understand that in the semblance of Berger's novel, radical contingency is norm rather than exception.

Had the owner of the hardware store in Dolf's town not recently committed suicide, Dolf would never have gone to Bud's store in Millville in the first place. Had he not been waited on by Bud's more or less rotten son, because Bud was busy talking to his cousin Reverton, the dispute about his unlit cigar would probably not have arisen. Had not Dolf initially mistaken Reverton first for a minister (reverend/Reverton), then for a policeman, the trajectory of the dispute would have been entirely different. Had cousin Reverton not been at the store and not been a classic paranoid who carried an unloaded track starter's pistol to give him an edge in disputes, then the initial disagreement could never have led to the kind of public humiliation that turns him against the entire Bullard family. All of this is precipitated on this particular day because Dolf decided to honor a promise made to his wife years before. And the feud is further escalated when Bullard's hardware store burns down that night, the fire actually started accidentally by Bullard's son but seen by the paranoid Reverton as an act of cowardly revenge by Dolf Beeler. Indeed, Berger's semblance is so complicated, and the sequence of its seemingly unconnected events so perversely woven together, that just to outline them takes great effort, the only accurate overview being that what happens, happens.

Of course, within two days Dolf gratuitously picks a fight with a coworker distantly related to the Bullard family and seems to win it only to suffer an eventually fatal heart attack, which might be reckoned a far more terrible experience, but one equally unbelievable—in life as in fiction—before it occurs. Moreover, this quiet-seeming novel swells with crucial and unexpected changes within the three days of its action. One of Dolf's sons,

Tony, stumbles into a feud-related vocation, going from assaulting one police chief to assisting another. Jack, his other son, makes a seemingly innocuous choice not to kiss a girl, but within the systems calculus of this novel, that choice may well be precisely the one that will eventually enable him to flee the narrowness of a small town for a career as a foreign correspondent. In short order, hardware-store owner Bud Bullard, one of Dolf's ostensible antagonists, sees his business destroyed by fire and suffers a nervous breakdown, but he adroitly seizes the first available opportunity to resurrect both store and psyche. Reverton, Bud's unfortunate cousin and the feud's primary architect, dies a hero in a shootout with a notorious bank robber. And Bud's malevolent son runs away from home, while Dolf's wonderfully pragmatic daughter sails through all manner of apparent reverses.

In it largest sense, Berger's title reminds us, as does this novel, that all of human life can be seen as a continuous feud with contingency, experience relentlessly refusing to conform to our expectations and explanations, our myths of existence refusing to acknowledge its disorder, our philosophical and epistemological maps ever at odds with the territories of actual living.

Harvey Yelton, chief of police in Hornbeck and another in a long line of Berger characters whose narrowness is so thoroughgoing as to give them a kind of wisdom, is the one character in this novel whose point of view may be broad enough to bring a sense of order to the seemingly disparate events that constitute *The Feud*'s plot. To Harvey, these events are quite unremarkable, since he pretty much views the world as a series of calamities waiting to happen. Driving down one of Hornbeck's streets, he sees a rubber ball roll across the street half a block ahead of him, pursued by a young boy of about ten. The chief stops his cruiser, gets out, and patiently lectures the boy:

Harvey said, "You know better than that, Willis. You oughtn't play ball so it comes into the street. You know why? It could hit somebody's automobile and scare them so they would lose control of the wheel and drive up over the curb and turn over and burst into flames, and everybody in the car would be burned to a crisp, see? Or the driver might just lose his head and turn and run over your pooch. Or you and your friends might tear after the ball onto the road and you'd all be killed if a big Mack truck was coming along real fast, or you'd scare the truckdriver and he'd smash into them high-tension wires, which would fall down and electrocute the whole neighborhood and kill everybody and burn up all your houses, maybe get outa control and burn everything in the whole town, see. Now, you wouldn't want that to happen, wouldja?" (67–68)

Harvey's description of an outrageously contingent world may strike us as a humorous example of rhetorical overkill—precisely the kind of thing adults resort to in their roles as authorities or officials when dealing with children—but he does, in fact, see the world in these terms, as in a sense must Berger, and as in a sense must all of us who experience the variety and vagaries of his novel.

A casual philanderer who exploits his power in every situation, Harvey is not a nice man, but he is an efficient small-town cop, and this passage goes far toward characterizing his "professional" point of view—one of fourteen distinct points of view presented in Berger's *Feud*. More important, however, he offers Berger's readers perhaps the only accurate map of, and key to, the sequence of events that make up the semblance of Berger's novel. For, outrageous as Harvey's hypothetical example may at first seem, it represents much more predictable and understandable sequences of events than does the action of *The Feud*. And it is the very unlikeliness of this action that signals that this may be Berger's most conventionally realistic work, one presenting the world as a place where things—good, bad, and inscrutable—happen quite independently of our intentions and expectations.

The one sure defense against contingency, in art as well as in life, is to readjust one's attitude in order to embrace or at least acknowledge unexpected developments, a cognitive remapping that changes the stories we tell ourselves in order to better correspond to ever-changing experience. The characters in all of Berger's novels are desperate practitioners of this strategy of cognitive remapping, although only a select few could be called its masters—among them Dolf Beeler's calculatingly promiscuous daughter, Bernice, one of Berger's most carefree survivors, who never considers the facts of her situation without subjecting them to the softening lens of self-interest. Considering her recent eviction, Bernice remaps her relationship with her ex-landlord:

He was a big fat greasy foreigner of some kind, with lots of hair in his nose and baggy eyes. Luckily he had never put a hand on her, or else she would have lambasted him with a hot curling iron, but if looks meant anything, he had done it to her plenty. She could have lived there rent-free for the rest of her life if she had given him a little of what he was dying for, but she was no tramp.

That's what hurt, when he called her one, though she should have considered the source and seen it was just sour grapes.

She had only smiled and said, "Maybe we can work something out till my ship comes in,"

"No danks," said he. "You see your sailors someplace else! Dis ain't no cat-houze.

Now you pull dat bathrobe shut, and den you pack up and get out inna morning."
(116)

The beauty of the above passage, and one of the sneaky attractions of
Berger's novel, is of course that as Bernice remaps the territory of her recent
experience, readers must remap the territory of their perception of Bernice.
And in ways both small and large, *The Feud* presents this remapping strategy
as perhaps the one constant in human nature. Certainly Berger ensures that it
becomes the one constant in our reading, as *The Feud* withholds crucial bits of
information or corrects the mistaken perceptions of its characters in ways that
compel us to resort to precisely the same kinds of cognitive remapping as
must its characters. The final implication of Berger's most rigorously systematic novel is that it makes the reader a participant in, rather than just a witness
to, its operations.

Neighbors

Berger writes that "[*Neighbors*] is my own favorite among my ten novels,
because at no point did I think consciously about it. It performed itself before
my eyes, without my intervention at any point: I served exclusively as specta-
tor. It is for me the absolutely pure fiction that I have lately aspired to, with
no taint of journalism, sociology, and the other corruptions" (23 May 1979).
If *Sneaky People* represents Berger's "tribute to the American language of
1939" as used by "the lower-middle class in the eastern Middle West," and if
The Feud echoes that tribute, allowing Berger to re-create the speech he heard
when a child, then *Neighbors* must surely represent, in part, a very different
kind of tribute to a very different kind of language—the leveled and banal
commonplaces of posttelevision homogenization. Not only does the action
of *Neighbors* consist primarily of functions of language but the characters,
particularly the confusing new neighbor Harry, rely almost exclusively on
commonplace phrases such as "face the music," "it's your word against mine,"
"take it like a man," "like a cornered rat," and "clutching at straws." While
agreeing on the relevancy of this observation, Berger has specified, "I made
no conscious effort to use cliches and commonplaces: these demonic characters produced them on their own volition, Harry especially" (4 September
1982). For his own purposes, however, Berger maintains a reasonable distinction between these two novels, explaining that "my own interest in writing
The Feud was linguistic, whereas for me *Neighbors* was a work in which the
preoccupation is with a man's life and death" (14 December 1987).

Neighbors may offer the most verbal world Berger has created; identifying the mode of this novel as his favorite, Berger describes it as "a creation and not the observation of existing reality" (30 July 81). Indeed, Berger's letters suggest again and again that this work held special significance for him: "*Neighbors* is rather like my plays, being mostly in dialogue and without the naturalistic detail and sociological pretext of the Reinhart books, but then I've been moving farther away from that in each novel. This is also my most artistically ambitious book and at the same time the one on which I shall have exerted the least effort of the usual, conscious kind. *Neighbors* is essentially automatic writing, created in a trance" (28 January 1979).

Berger's protagonist for this delightfully perplexing novel, Earl Keese, a quiet, reasonable forty-nine-year-old suburbanite, tells people that his home sits "at the end of the road," because that construction sounds less "dispiriting" than "at a dead end." But when Harry and Ramona move next door, within twenty-four hours Keese is faced with a sequence of situations so outrageous that he can find no rhetorical constructions to mask their threat or to maintain the hoax of his previously complacent life.

Mysterious and maddening, Harry and Ramona are, by turns, forward, friendly, rude, flattering, insulting, provoking, and threatening. Their words and actions are always unexpected and usually contradictory. For instance, when Keese first responds to Ramona's knock at his door and phatically asks her, "And what may I do for you?" her response is a most disconcerting "Anything you like. . . . The problem is what you want in return." More and more, the visits of Harry and Ramona seem like assaults. Their random comings and goings produce a series of off-balance events, each more preposterous than the last, gradually stripping Keese of his easy assumptions and habitual responses—not to mention his clothing.

Madcap physical changes punctuate Berger's plot—entrances, exits, searches, fights, a damaged car, a destroyed house, even a sudden death—but for all its action, *Neighbors* might best be described as a series of functions of language: puns, platitudes, commonplaces, theories, definitions, excuses, accusations, rationalizations, promises, questions, threats—all acts performed with words. Keese, Berger has commented, "is a prisoner of what he believes to be his responsibilities, in language as in all else."[8] Keese responds to what the world says it is doing, rather than to what it actually does, and this makes him the perfect target of Ramona's and Harry's verbal hoaxes. They hoax him intermittently, but language itself hoaxes him continuously.

Harry and Ramona seem committed to tweaking Keese's sensibility, to pushing him to see how far he will go to avoid humiliation, to pestering, haunting, and ultimately rearranging his life. Their decidedly unneighborly behavior stuns him, placing him at such disadvantage in all his dealings with them that he is driven to respond in thoughts and actions even more outlandish than theirs. "Maybe I'm just testing you," Ramona cryptically observes, while all Keese can do is desperately sigh, "I am trying to adjust to a life in which chance encounters can be brutal" (125).

In this absurdly skewed context, Harry's firing a shotgun at Keese and offering him an obviously dirty coffee cup seem equally offensive, and Harry and Ramona sting Keese as much by accusing him of sarcasm as they do by falsely accusing him of attempted rape. Their behavior is so confusing, in part, because they keep shifting among the registers of social and linguistic codes—responding to the code of friendship with that of a feud, responding literally to figurative statements, refusing to speak or act on Keese's wavelength. And by refusing to comply with these codes of speech and action, they call attention to the arbitrary and essentially phatic patterns that govern so much of human interchange. Once these patterns have been exposed and their tenuous nature revealed by simple refusals to speak or act "right," the concept of right itself seems more and more problematic, and in this crucible of paradoxes and contradictions, Earl must distill a new behavioral code to guide his actions—a new morality that in its complexity must follow Nietzsche "beyond good and evil."

As Keese's experiences increasingly blur the lines between comedy and nightmare and between hallucination and reality, his relations with all those around him begin to undergo subtle changes—a metamorphosis. He realizes that his life has grown so stale that Harry's and Ramona's crazy-seeming aggravations may actually offer him a salvation of sorts—the chance to take control of, and give style to, his life, to team up with them and "roam the boulevards with a supercilious smile for all, and glide through smart shops exchanging glib remarks." In a fundamental sense, Harry and Ramona reveal to him the meaning of freedom. And this change is not beyond Keese's notice, as he finally admits to Harry, "Every time I see you as a criminal, by another light you look like a kind of benefactor" (259). Like almost all of Berger's protagonists, Keese has been imprisoned by his own elaborate codes of responsibility, fairness, and decency, terms that seem to have no meaning for, much less control over, the actions of Harry and Ramona. As surely as Keese's outrage over the seeming pecadilloes of his new neighbors grows dangerously, even pathologically, violent, chinks begin to appear in his moral armor. His initial impatience with "the philosophies which disregarded the problem of guilt" soon gives way to the realization that "it's easy to excuse everything in some way. . . . For example, murder can be seen in one light as merely getting rid of someone—as a mere removal" (127). It falls to his wife,

Enid, to put things in perspective for him with her blunt explanation for her own questionable conduct. "What's morality have to do with it?" she asks. "I'm speaking of self-preservation" (223).

And so is Berger, but in a most subtle and complicated fashion, along lines explored in one way or another by Pierre de Laclos, Nietzsche, Kafka, and Berger himself in his three plays. Part of Berger's achievement in *Neighbors* is that he has subsumed the traditions of these three writers within his own uniquely ironic style. Indeed, the best joke in *Neighbors* is that beneath its slapstick action and farcical humor lies a very serious investigation of the relationship between freedom and victimization.

Anyone familiar with Berger's novels knows his longstanding fascination with the question "who is kicker and who kickee," but it is not generally known that Berger has most directly confronted this issue in his plays. Around 1969 Berger tried his hand a playwriting, completing three plays, all unpublished (one of them, however, *Other People*, was produced in 1970 at the Berkshire Theatre Festival in Massachusetts). Each of them (the other two are *The Siamese Twins* and *Rex, Rita, and Roger*) involves the ways in which definitions of self determine power relationships, and each develops a sense of paranoia out of seemingly absurd situations. *Rex, Rita, and Roger*, and *The Siamese Twins* seem to present almost a situational blueprint for *Neighbors*, both plays vexing a static domestic scene by introducing ominous outsiders.

Rex, Rita, and Roger investigates the nature of will through a farcical confrontation more than a little reminiscent of that in Melville's "Bartleby the Scrivener." Rex brings home to Rita, his wife, a man he has found in the subway. The man, Roger, is apparently incapable of exercising his will, and Rex sees in him a perfect pseudo-slave: since Roger has no will, he is completely compliant with Rex's suggestions and cannot be considered a slave only because he has no will to do other than what Rex demands. But while he may not have a will, Roger does possess skills. In his responses to questions he reveals an impressive command of *gourmandise*, and Rex and Rita decide that he will make a wonderful combination chef-maître d'. At their first dinner party, however, Roger's expertise quickly shades into derision of their culinary ignorance and then into taking complete charge of their and their guest's actions. After a number of absurd confrontations, Rex regains control both of the situation and of his household, and his regaining of ascendancy is matched by certain gains in understanding. Rita notes that ever since Roger came into their house, Rex has "turned into quite the philosopher," while Rex notes that Roger has managed to free him from a lot of pressures. The pattern of the play raises many of the same issues more obliquely addressed by Bartleby's paradoxical relationship with his employer, the main difference being that Berger presents the victim-victimizer relationship as necessarily cyclical and potentially enlightening: through their reciprocal master-slave roles, both Rex and Roger come to a new understanding of their need for each other.

The rough situational similarities between *Rex, Rita, and Roger* and *Neighbors* are nothing, however, when compared with those between *Neighbors* and *The Siamese Twins*. In the latter play, two new neighbors, "large, blond, and beautiful" Siamese twins—Robert and Roberta—descend upon the unquiet suburban household of Leo, his wife Phylis, and her transvestite brother, Francis. In much the style later employed by Harry and Ramona, these twins defy all the established social codes and immediately begin to critique and to disrupt Leo's household. Apart from the exotic fact that they have been joined at the hip by a band of flesh, Robert and Roberta seem linked in some vague therapeutic enterprise. They refer to themselves as useful intermediaries with an unbroken record of successes, and they wonder whether there may be others "in greater need" than Leo, Phylis, and Francis. "Who are you people? Where do you get the nerve to march into my house and take over?" screams Leo. As is true of *Neighbors, The Siamese Twins* consists of a series of absurd actions that are almost exclusively functions of language: accusations, criticisms, apologies, clichés, coaching, and commentary. Roberta and Robert seem determined to shock the members of the household into a kind of regression therapy. Their unpredictable antics completely restructure the dynamics of the relationships among Leo, Phylis, and Francis, but when the maddened Francis grabs a knife and cuts through the band of flesh that has joined them, Robert and Roberta begin to realize a number of flaws in their own seemingly harmonious existence. As is true of so many of Berger's dramatic situations, radically changed perspectives completely undermine the seemingly clear distinctions between victim and victimizer.

Like Robert and Roberta, Harry and Ramona of *Neighbors* seem more than a little reminiscent of Nietzsche's "blond brute," his prototypical "free spirit" (Earl explicitly describes them as "free spirits," while Ramona says, "We're just a pair of shiftless zanies"). Certainly, the conflict between Earl and his new neighbors seems to dramatize the conflict described by Nietzsche as that between "slave," or "herd," and "master" moralities. Earl's initially submissive behavior, his obsession with proper form, his growing sense of resentment, even his elaborate and violent imaginary retaliations, make him an almost perfect model for Nietzsche's man of ressentiment. The toothy and tawny Harry and Ramona flaunt their rudeness and their ungoverned instinct—both virtues in the Nietzschean scheme of things, both signs of an honest animality. Read in this manner, *Neighbors* becomes almost a dramatization (some might say a burlesque) of Nietzsche's views of universal "neighborliness." It is Nietzsche who argues that fear and the will to power are what really structure relationships between humans, and he even specifies that it is fear of the neighbor that gives rise to "new perspectives of moral valuation." In what seems even more specifically the tone of Berger's novel, Nietzsche states: "The striving for excellence is the striving to overwhelm one's neighbor. . . . The striving for excellence brings with it *for the neighbor*—to name only a few steps of this long ladder: tortures, then blows, then terror, then anguished amazement, then wonder, then envy, then laughing, then ridicule, then derision, then scorn, then the dealings of blows, then the inflicting of tortures."[9] A better description of the action of *Neighbors* would be hard to find.

If the world of *Neighbors* seems remarkably like that depicted in Nietzsche's philosophy, it also should be noted that it has much in common with that of two novels: Kafka's *Trial* and Laclos's *Dangerous Acquaintances*. While the epistolary form of Laclos's masterpiece is, if at all, only faintly suggested by the great emphasis placed in Berger's novel on disastrously funny telephone calls, both books create almost exclusively verbal worlds in which no two perspectives of an event ever agree and in which motivation is almost never what it seems. The nature of the relationship between Harry and Ramona seems as unorthodox and as unstable as that between Laclos's Valmont and Madame de Merteuil, both pairs of victimizers become victims themselves, and both pairs seem to exist only on the axis of dominance and subordination. Both novels suggest (although in quite different terms) that alienation is a necessary step on the way to personal freedom. Substitute the Nietzschean concept of the will to power for Laclos's concept of the will to evil and the resemblance between *Neighbors* and *Dangerous Acquaintances* becomes even more pronounced.

Berger's homage to Kafka, from whom he learned that "at any moment banality might turn sinister, for existence was not meant to be unfailingly genial," is clearer still.[10] Vocabularies from law and ethics intertwine throughout *Neighbors*, and Berger does not fail to exploit the incongruities of the two lexicons. Terms having to do with guilt, justice, punishment, revenge, motive, confession, defense, blame, crime, accusation, etc., appear on virtually every page of this novel, resonating at once with the rhetoric of the courtroom and with that of Kafka's *Trial*. In fact, one accurate summary of the action of *Neighbors* would be that it is a series of mock trials, in a legal sense, all of which serve as a trial for Keese's patience and ultimately for his worldview. That Berger's protagonist is another "K." is no accident, nor is Keese's "guilt" unlike that of Kafka's Joseph K.

But just as surely as Berger invokes the verbal worlds of Kafka or Nietzsche or Booth Tarkington, his style radically transforms those worlds, his irony setting up a dizzying dialectic. In *Neighbors,* as is the case for most, if not all, of Berger's novels, that irony functions on at least three conceptual levels, ironic layers located in the reading of the novels, in the place of language in the lives of his characters, and in the situations of life in general—experience common to both readers and characters. For the reader of these novels, a mild irony lies in the recognition of Berger's celebration of earlier literary traditions, a subtle tweaking of forms that is in itself funny. More directly, Berger's narrative continually highlights the ironic ways in which the worlds of his characters' language are exposed as being at odds with the worlds of their experience. And finally, the lives of those characters suggest not only that the joke implicit in imaginative literature mirrors a larger joke in the human condition but that death itself is but the ultimate irony. For Buddy Sandifer in *Sneaky People,* as for Dolf Beeler and Reverton in *The Feud* and for Earl Keese in *Neighbors,* death "could happen to anybody" and does—proving to be the sneakiest experience of all, always the final irony.

The Houseguest

For readers familiar with Berger's writing, just the title of his fifteenth novel, *The Houseguest* (1988), suffices to invoke dialectically opposed expectations. The example of *Neighbors* and of Berger's plays strongly suggests that a work so titled will surely involve the imposition of a mysterious and threatening outsider—the houseguest—on a static, if not enervated, domestic situation. The outsider can be expected somehow to gain power, moral authority, over the family whose hospitality he or she takes advantage of, recasting the guest-host relationship in terms of Berger's favored paradigm of kicker-kickee. This dominance, however, may ultimately prove chimerical, beneficial, or both—revealing or clarifying to the ostensible victims basic truths of their existence. Yet, much as this pattern is to be expected, the body of Berger's writing suggests even more strongly that the expected is precisely what his fiction refuses to be. From this dialectic emerges a novel at once surprisingly predictable and predictably surprising, testimony to the consistency of Berger's originality as well as to the steadiness of his vision.

In Berger's view, *The Houseguest,* like *Neighbors* before it, is "mostly a creation and not the observation of existing reality" (30 July 1981). The author, who began writing this novel as early as 1981, has also described it as a story "in which the title-character arrived at nobody's invitation and dominated everybody in the house, resisted only by the daughter-in-law," a narrative he accurately judges "reminiscent of *Neighbors* only in the relentlessness of the idea" (28 Jan 1982). Indeed, in its emphasis on the arrogant superficiality of class and the trappings of money, its presentation of a mysterious outsider with no known history, and in the sterile relationships among its five principal characters, Berger's novel might best be regarded as an abstracted, twisted, and desentimentalized parallel to *The Great Gatsby.*

At the intersection of *The Houseguest*'s surprising and predictable aspects is the fact that for the first time in Berger's novels, his narrative focus falls on a woman. Female characters have long been the centers of pragmatism and strength in Berger's fiction—the only characters who seem regularly to know their goals, much less accomplish them—but their points of view have rarely been sustained. *Arthur Rex* poses a major exception to this rule, but even there Berger's women, while emerging as perhaps the most interesting characters in the Arthurian story, are finally overshadowed by the mythic power of the male-centered legend. The multiple inversions of *Regiment of Women* also complicate generalizations about Berger's female characters by presenting a woman's point of view for a male character, but only in the service of rejecting the rhetoric of gender. *The Houseguest* unequivocally presents a female protagonist, both the primary narrative focus of the novel and the primary actor in its events. That Berger's protagonist is a woman, however, does not become clear before the end of the novel, as she only gradually distinguishes herself in our consciousness, emerging as the one character capable of growth and deserving of our respect. Even more surprising, these obviously admirable qualities do not seem to preclude success, as Berger's protagonist proves at least the temporary winner in her various conflicts with the houseguest and her prominent and socially conscious in-laws.

The first sentence is one of Berger's most informatively outrageous openings, positing as it does a number of seemingly unreasonable propositions: "The process that led to the decision to kill Chuck Burgoyne, who for the first week of his visit had proved the perfect houseguest, began on Sunday when, though he had promised to prepare breakfast for all (he was a superb cook), he had not yet appeared in the kitchen by half past noon" (3). "Process" is the key word here, as Berger explores the innumerable processes by which people adhere to codes of behavior without understanding or agreeing with the teleology of those codes.

So adroit is this Chuck Burgoyne at playing the role of the perfect houseguest that the Graves family initially fails to realize that he is not only uninvited to their isolated summer home on an island but is unknown to any of them, each mistakenly believing Chuck to be the friend of another family member. The mere fact that Chuck can cook distinguishes him from his hosts, a distinction accentuated by his general competence in all areas, a competence that quickly comes to seem ominous. Lydia's new family proves accomplished only in negative respects: Doug as a cynical philanderer, Audrey as a discrete alcoholic, and Bobby as a paragon of fecklessness. Resentment, toward each other and the world at large, is all they have in common, and their grim focus on rituals of hospitality is all that holds the family together.

Having insinuated himself into their routine as a kind of social glue, the one standard on which all can agree, Chuck then drops his accommodating mask, engaging in a series of transgressive acts, ranging from his failure to prepare breakfast to his rape of Lydia as she sleeps, exhausted from nearly drowning in an undertow from which Chuck has saved her and about which the family had neglected to warn her. Perhaps his most serious transgression is honesty, as his appraisals of his antagonists are brutally frank but not inaccurate: " 'There's a lot of deceit in this house,' Chuck said. 'That's what strikes me as a guest: how much you all lie to one another. Unless you're all simply that insensitive and unobservant' " (95).

Chuck's honesty eventually complicates our reading when it turns toward Bobby, Lydia's new husband. When Lydia informs Bobby that Chuck has raped her, he simply does not believe her; when Chuck smugly confirms that charge, Bobby simply cannot believe his own ears and thinks himself the victim of a terrible delusion. Chuck incredulously comments: "You're virtually an idiot, aren't you? In a poorer family you'd be kept at home and given a little yardwork to do, trimming the edges, raking leaves, et cetera. They wouldn't let you marry and pass on your inferior genes" (134). Little if any evidence in the novel challenges this view, and yet Lydia has lived with, married, and professes to love the object of Chuck's derision. The challenge to the reader here is to decide whether Chuck's view (pretty much seconded by Bobby's parents) is compelling and, if it is, to decide whether Lydia's marriage rests on cynical or opportunistic grounds or whether her love for Bobby is profound, a sign of almost saintly understanding.

Revealing himself to be a relative of the ubiquitous Finches, brutish locals (surely a branch of the notorious Greavy family in *Neighbors*) who provide all the services for the Graves family, Chuck easily takes over the household, intimidating without actually threatening, contemptuously exposing their desperate confusion of class with character, of money with moral strength. At the point when the family comes closest to murdering him, rationalizing their actions as self-defense, Chuck has probably not even broken any laws. Recognizing that Lydia alone has the spirit to oppose him, he tells her of his victory that it "was like knocking overripe fruit off a tree. It is *too* easy. I wish I could get a challenge out of somebody, but they're such worms" (149).

Although Chuck correctly perceives that Lydia is not like the rest of the
Graves family, he incorrectly believes that she has more than that difference
in common with him. The crucial distinction, Lydia informs him, is that
while he is "nothing but a cheap hustler," she is "trying to accomplish something here." Not only does she resist his opportunism but she also eventually
wrests away from him his power over the family. From her initial determination, however, to assume responsibility for avenging her rape, Lydia grows to
recognize a larger responsibility for her surroundings, which means that she
decides to assume Chuck's former power, but to use it for the moral education and betterment of the Graves family. "We're going to make good use of
the rest of the summer, despite this bad start," she firmly announces (229).
The former houseguest is retained as a new family employee, while Lydia demands and receives the rights and privileges accorded to a houseguest. Yielding completely to her authority, her father-in-law grudgingly accepts her as "a
necessary evil, like a policeman."

Lydia's victory may or may not last. Her spirit and moral vitality have
carried the day, but with considerable assistance from a large caliber police
revolver. She has not been "contaminated" (her word) by her new environment, but her new designation as houseguest, while signifying a potential
gain in privilege, also seems to represent a distinctly pragmatic
rearrangement of her marriage and an unmistakable step toward a marriage
such as that of her in-laws. More important, the central irony of Chuck's
brief dominance, an irony implicit in his bitter claim to the family that
"there's never been anything you could supply that I would want," now
would seem to become Lydia's burden as well. The four benign smiles she
sees as the novel closes can hardly seem reassuring.

There is simply no describing the complex and shifting moral equations
worked through in each of this novel's scenes, but something of the book's
movement and of Lydia's moral development can be seen in its overarching
chiastic structure. Not only do Lydia and Chuck exchange positions of power
and the title of houseguest but a more abstract ethical switch guides the process of that exchange. After saving Lydia from an undertow, Chuck claims
sovereignty over her, both physically and morally: she owes him her life. And
even though outraged by his violation of her body, Lydia acquiesces in this invocation of a primitive code, feeling completely free to depose him only after
she saves his life (even, in complete reciprocity, saving him from drowning),
thus equalling the score. Her reaction to saving the family from Chuck's
domination, however, both invokes and inverts that same code of responsibility, as she now sees herself responsible for them, rather than them obligated to
her. "Don't you understand that now it's up to me to make something of you

people, now that I've saved you from Chuck?" (230). Lydia has negotiated the transition from insecure outsider to person in charge, but her success has been at the considerable cost of accepting new responsibility—at once the bane of all of Berger's characters, and their triumph.

Chapter Seven
Celebrations of Style
Fundamental Patterns in Berger's Novels

Unifying the apparent diversity of Thomas Berger's fifteen novels is his thoroughgoing fascination with the many dimensions of prose style, appearing as they do in the languages of life as well as those of literature. This fascination with language gives rise to all the fundamental patterns of Berger's fiction, informing the basic structure, themes, and character portrayals in his novels. As a result, his fiction challenges us to recognize that we live more in a world of words than of things, a condition where the mechanisms of language—the ways in which we think and talk about existence—determine the quality of experience more than do the "facts" of experience themselves. Indeed, as character after character encounters (but does not often learn) in Berger's novels, the very idea of a "fact" is a linguistic rather than sensory phenomenon, and as such it can be manipulated and distorted, usually to someone's specific ends, to the detriment of someone else. For example, even his remarkable ability to become invisible does not free *Being Invisible*'s Fred Wagner, from the petty tyranny of a doctor who insists, "Let's move step by step from what we can establish as veritable fact and try to avoid epistemological tricks by which *je pense* can pretend to be proof that *je suis*" (228). Confronted with the apparent fact of an X-ray in which Wagner's internal organs seem to be missing, the doctor simply douses this fire of the fantastic with language, calmly musing, "I will 'grant' to use your term though it's hardly apropos, only that I was not able to see them just now with the fluoroscope."

This is but one in a series of recurring situations in Berger's novels in which language seems to war with "reality." Or, more properly, the situation reminds us that whatever the physical, experiential terrain of "reality," we know that sensory terrain primarily from the map of language—a map continuously redrawn to suit the selfish interests of the mapmakers in all of us. Berger's novels call attention to this phenomenon as it operates in the form of the novel itself, as well as in the lives of his characters. One way of summarizing this overriding concern is simply to say that for Berger, the novel's most profound subject must always be the power of language.

Of course, Berger is not alone in his exploration of the wonders and vagaries of language, and the consideration of his novels should acknowledge the larger context of the self-reflexive tendencies of recent literature—but only as a prelude to distinguishing Berger's unique concerns and techniques. We need to consider the nature of Berger's celebrations of classic genres, to suggest their paratactic structure, to identify the ways in which he makes language his primary theme, to show how this shapes his characters, and, finally, to establish the importance of Nietzsche for any sophisticated understanding of Berger's novels.

Berger and the Self-reflexive Tradition

Some years ago President Lyndon Johnson, himself a master at creating political fictions, admitted that he did not like to read literary fiction because it *was not true.* In Berger's *Sneaky People,* young Ralph Sandifer expresses much the same outraged conviction after his epiphany that a piece of pornography was not, as it purported to be, a factual account of experience. "This book was fiction; which was to say, pure crap from beginning to end about nothing that had actually happened or that really mattered" (254). Many of the novels written in the last fifteen or twenty years have echoed this concern, although for quite different reasons and to quite different ends. Indeed, it has become the norm for experimental literature to be self-reflexively confessional, experimenting primarily with ways of reminding the reader that fiction is not only "not true" but also "not real," that the world of words is radically split from the world of objects. Such confessions, however, show defiance rather than contrition, arguing that "fiction is artifice, but not artificial," and claiming for the novel a nonmimetic, even nonrepresentational role. Roland Barthes has suggested that the goal of these efforts is "to substitute the instance of discourse for the instance of reality (or of the referent)."[1]

Put another way, the goal is to shift our attention, from a purportedly real world we live in, to the ways in which that world is conventionally perceived as a construct of language. This effort proceeds from the assumption that what we have been told about reality (received ideas) and what we tell ourselves about reality (our personal myths) have become more "official" or persuasive than experience itself, that language has been so twisted, so manipulated as to refer more to itself than to the material world to which it ostensibly refers. It is in this sense that Berger cheerfully warns that we should not confuse fiction with life, because "*the latter* is false," and it is in this spirit that he reminds the readers of *Killing Time* that his novel "is a construction of language and otherwise a lie."

Whether or not one subscribes to the suspicion of, and fascination with, language that has largely dominated twentieth century philosophy and literature, it provides a context in which Berger's writing must be considered. And in that context the reader should understand that Berger's novels, no matter how realistic they may seem, are anything but examples of literary realism. No matter how traditional their invocation of literary genres seems, they soon radically restructure those genres; no matter how conventional their writing may at first appear, that writing is profoundly innovative.

The Paratactic Celebration of Classic Novel Genres

The self-ironizing metafictional orientation of much recent American literature provides a useful background for the consideration of some of the major structuring concerns in Berger's novels, although Berger's literary experiments stem from different assumptions and proceed toward different ends than do those of the more avowedly metafictional writers. In this sense, Berger's writing has much more in common with that of Borges and Nabokov than with that of Barth and Robert Coover. The fictions of all three writers are distinctly self-reflexive, but in a spirit of play (what Nabokov called "aesthetic bliss") more than in the service of any polemic of literary theory. In fact, because Berger's fiction never advertises its anomalies, seeming to follow conventional narrative patterns, linear time schemes, and standard syntax, its experimental or innovative dimension has been usually overlooked. In this respect, Berger's style somewhat resembles the broad pattern of deception best explained by Poe's Inspector Dupin, a theory explicitly invoked by one of the major characters in Berger's first novel, *Crazy in Berlin*. Interpreting a cryptic letter from a childhood friend, Schild remembers Dupin's theory of deception in Poe's "Purloined Letter." Referring to a map puzzle in which one player requires another to find the name of a certain town, Dupin explains that while the novice will invariably choose the most minutely lettered names, "the adept selects such words as stretch, in large characters, from one end of the chart to the other," because these words "escape observation by being excessively obvious" (211).

Berger's literary experiments are of this large-letter kind, sneaky in their obviousness. To recognize that this so-obvious-as-to-be-overlooked experimental aspect is a major feature of Berger's style, the reader must understand the nature of his celebrations of classic novel genres. The jacket note written by Berger for *Who is Teddy Villanova?* reviews the general scheme of his career: "Each of Thomas Berger's novels celebrates another classic genre of fiction: the western (*Little Big Man*), the childhood memoir (*Sneaky People*), the anatomical romance (*Regiment of Women*), the true-crime documentary (*Killing Time*), and the Reinhart books (*Crazy in Berlin, Reinhart in Love, and Vital Parts*) together form a sociological epic."

Who is Teddy Villanova? extends this pattern to the classic American hard-boiled detective story, and *Arthur Rex* to Arthurian romance; *Neighbors* traces its lineage to Kafka, Laclos, and Sade; and *Reinhart's Women* continues the sociological epic of the Reinhart series. Berger describes his twelfth novel, *The Feud*, as a "Dreiserian slice of life," while *Nowhere*, his thirteenth, clearly invokes the utopian/dystopian tradition of Swift and Butler. *Being Invisible*, Berger's fourteenth published novel, has ties to H. G. Wells's and Ralph Ellison's quite different invisible men, while *The Houseguest* presents a self-made hollow man in the tradition of *The Great Gatsby* (although Berger suggests that this novel may have had its origins in a John Belushi skit on "Saturday Night Live").

The notion that these books parody their genre forms has dogged Berger's career, appearing in most reviews of his work. However, the careful study of genre sources that has preceded the writing of these novels has been for Berger too much a labor of love to result only in parody. Unlike parody, Berger's novels start from, rather than aim toward, the traditions of literary formulas, a testing and broadening of possibilities rather than a burlesquing of limitations. Berger has explained: "I never think about form. The structure of any book of mine comes from the sequence of the words. My conscious intention is always to write as conventional an example (of whichever genre) as I can manage to do. Thus I never begin with the intention to deride a genre; my purpose is always to celebrate it, to identify and applaud its glories" (11 February 1977). While he goes on to admit, "I am usually hoodwinked by my imagination before I get far," that imagination looks far beyond the conventions of literary genres. In a recent interview with Richard Schickel, Berger expressed his impatience with those who mistake him "for a merry-andrew with an inflated pig's bladder," because such readers "can never understand that I adore whichever tradition I am striving to follow, and that what results is the best I can manage by way of joyful worship—not the worst in sneering derision."[2]

I take Berger at his word here, for the simple reason that the underlying concern in his novels with the role of language clearly stems from interests more significant than those of literary form. If anything, his celebrations serve as kinds of "de-parodisations," twisting genres, already self-conscious to the point of parody, in ways that radically defamiliarize them. It seems to me that in their largest contours his celebrations of literary genres function in much the same way as do the graphics of M. C. Escher. Escher's *Autre Monde*

provides a particularly useful visual paradigm for considering the design of a
Berger novel.

Autre Monde presents a bizarre fantasy moonscape haunted by metallic-
looking birds with human faces. We view these birds through the impossibly
connected arches of a Mobius cathedral. Escher's cathedral appears to break
physical laws by following the arbitrary conventions of perspective so rigorously
that they become absurd, yielding a world that looks correct when examined
part by part but that is impossible when viewed as a whole. E. H. Gombrich
has explained the consequences of Escher's technique. "It is only when we come
to look more closely that we see such a structure cannot exist in our world and
that the artist wants to transpose us into the giddy realms where terms such as
'up' and 'down' and 'right' and 'left' have lost their meaning. The print is an
artist's meditation on space, but it is also a demonstration of the beholder's
share; it is in trying to work out the intended relation of things and sights that
we realize the paradoxes of his arrangement."[3]

Like Escher, Berger creates a world where conventions of arrangement are
pursued so rigorously that they reveal their inadequacies, establishing a verbal world as impossible and as perplexing as the visual worlds of Escher's
graphics. For him this involves pursuing linguistic and literary codes in combinations or to extremes that turn traditional patterns of literary order to new
ends. Some indication of his technique may be seen in the way Berger discusses his use of irony. "I am ironic, by which I mean I endeavor to show how
things *are* as opposed to what they are generally thought to be. I am, in fact,
so ironic that often I pursue the inquiry until it turns back and reveals that
that which has been exposed as illusion or delusion is actually true."[4] Berger's
most enduring character, Carlo Reinhart, expressed a similar conviction in
Crazy in Berlin, describing irony as "that means to confront the ideal with the
actual and not go mad, that whip which produced the pain that hurts-so-
good, so that in the measure to which it hurt it was also funny. Finally, having
flogged and laughed yourself to the rim of death's trench, you looked within
and saw irony's own irony: the last truth was the first" (247–248).

What makes Berger's experiments with literary traditions hard to detect is
that, like Escher, he follows the rules of conventional arrangement, but he
may do so through a paratactic jumble of literary codes. "What finally
emerges from the work of so many 'experimental' writers is utter banality—
the elaborate acrobatics end with the performer on his feet, bowing to the audience," Berger has noted. "I think that what I say implicitly to the reader is:
'Let's pretend that the law of gravity has *not* been abrogated.' I am often confused with those writers who advertise their own annulment of such a law and

invite all comers to join the celebration. But I am not really a lawbreaker. I do all I can to preserve order" (8 November 1976).

It should be observed, however, that the "order" preserved by Berger is hardly that with which his novels begin. Rather it is the order of an Escher print, utilizing the old rules or conventions, but in a way that forces us to look at them and not just through them, and to reconsider their implications for our perception. In *Autre Monde*, Escher does not break any of the "rules" of depiction: he does not ignore the conventions of perspective, nor does he break down his picture into its conceptual components, as might a cubist. Yet his picture is impossible, nonrational. It reminds us that we are not just viewing an impossible world but a *picture* of an impossible scene. This reflexive quality of his art, its tendency to call attention to its own artifice, is best seen in another of his well-known prints, in which one hand (A) is drawing another hand (B), which in turn is drawing still another hand (A). One result of this kind of reflexivity is that it makes us conscious of the different frames of reference through which we view his scenes and his pictures. What Escher brings out is that strict use of conventional representations of reality can create from fragmented elements a seemingly real picture with no relation to the experiential world. These graphics resist passive observation, challenging us as beholders not only to work out the paradoxes of Escher's visual arrangements but also to form some attitude toward the visual riddles and revelations that confront us. To figure out *what* an Escher print is about takes little effort, but to figure out *why* it exists in its peculiar form is both the beholder's task and treat.

Berger's novels characteristically do much the same thing. What Berger terms the "alternative reality" or "independent existence" of his novel is a verbal world that both owes its existence to a number of traditional and arbitrary conventions of representation and seeks to remind us that the artificiality of these conventions is of interest and significance in itself—not just as a means to the representation of reality. Berger's persistent reminders throughout his novels "that a work of fiction is a construction of language and otherwise a lie" emerge primarily from some kind of parataxis. Rhetorical parataxis is the syntax of putting clauses together in a sentence without trying to relate them hierarchically. Literary parataxis extends this syntax to the larger structures and themes of the novel, juxtaposing seemingly incongruous sentences, narrative codes, and other forms or concepts within the text. This parataxis only rarely appears at the level of Berger's sentences, which seem both syntactically and semantically normal. Instead, it usually occurs in broader patterns of adherence to, and divergence from, literary formulas, and exists in the unexplained and unexpected combination of conventions from very different literary traditions, revealing itself only to readers with considerable literary sophistication. Unexpected kinds of parataxis allow Berger to intensify the inherently and consistently dialectical manner of his style. What is so remarkable is that the synthesis of Berger's fiction emerges, not from the straightforward conflict of opposing views, but ever from the radically oblique syntax of the paratactic.

The most obvious example of Berger's use of this technique is probably *Who is Teddy Villanova?*, in which he places side by side the landmarks of the American hard-boiled private-detective story and a protagonist who speaks (as another character pointedly observes!) "as though quoting Macaulay." The parataxis in that novel exists in the disparate literary formulas it invokes, as well as at the level of its sentences, which wildly swing back and forth from street vernacular to an ornateness and intricacy so refined as to make an English professor blush.

Much more subtle and conceptual forms of parataxis can be found in Berger's other novels and form one of the significant continuities of his style. This formal parataxis serves to turn familiar literary patterns into unexpected means to self-reflexive ends, denying or inverting our attendant expectations about what those literary patterns usually mean. Accordingly, we quickly recognize familiar formula landmarks—say of the historical novel in *Little Big Man* or of the hard-boiled detective story in *Who is Teddy Villanova?* —in Berger's novels, but that recognition comes with significant differences, like seeing an old friend suddenly gone cheerfully insane or an old insane friend cheerfully restored to reason. The effect of Berger's "strange-making" is to pursue formula conventions past the point of their emblematic meaning to the point where they must assume a fresh, particular meaning within the context of his novel only. His paratactic structure functions, in part, to redirect our concern from the story told by his fiction to the story that *is* his fiction itself.

Berger's parataxis is of systems or patterns within the text, and my references to genre and formula indicate the usually abstract nature of these patterns. My claim that Berger's structure is essentially paratactic rests on three such abstract patterns. The first of these has to do with the form of the novel itself, as Berger paratactically combines disparate, if not antithetical, literary genres, traditions, and conventions in his celebrations of classic novel forms. The second kind of paratactic patterning in his novels occurs in the language of his narrators and characters, in the form of wild shifts of register—the kinds of language they use. And the final paratactic pattern emerges from the situations of his characters as they encounter unexpected and incongruous shifts in their experience of culture—the stereotypes and codes of conduct of their society. Although no rigorous distinction among these levels can be maintained, I mean by them simply that Berger juxtaposes in his novels cultural stereotypes, linguistic codes, and literary formulas in unexpected ways. Having invoked the literary code of a particular novel form, he may well people his novel with characters who use language in ways associated with quite different genres. Having invoked a cultural stereotype in drawing a character, he may give that character attributes of thought and speech seemingly at odds with the stereotype.

For example, *Little Big Man* combined formula elements from the traditional western with those from Nabokovian tour de force, giving us the stereotype of the frontier hero but undercutting that stereotype with the sophisticated self-consciousness of his narration. In the same manner, *Regiment of Women* so mixed sexual stereotyping with linguistic and literary codes that it managed to miff readers on both sides of the women's rights issue, blinding many readers and reviewers alike to the fact that Berger's real concern in that novel was with the vagaries of language rather than with those of sexuality. More recently, Berger's *Being Invisible* invoked the fantastic premises of the literature and film of invisibility, only to demonstrate that even invisibility is no counter to banality and petty humiliation. In each case, Berger constructed his novels in unexpected ways from unexpected combinations of literary, linguistic, and cultural codes, ever reminding us of the insidious determinism of our expectations.

The Theme of Language

To observe that Berger's style characteristically employs kinds of formal parataxis and to note the self-reflexive import of that parataxis is, however, not to suggest that metafictional reflexivity is Berger's goal any more than is parody. While his technique would seem to align him with novelists such as Barth who are trying to redefine the role of the novel, Berger's primary concern is, not with literature, but with language. John Leonard has admired Berger for the way he "uses the English language as a trampoline,"[5] a description that is both accurate and a bit misleading. Certainly, one of the distinguishing features of Berger's writing is his highlighting of language, hovering as it often does on the verge of tour de force. His sentences twist syntax, display exotic diction, and sharpen his thoughts and images toward ever more precise edges. Berger's mastery of his prose style, however, does not mean that his attitude toward language is that of a craftsman toward his tools. Instead, the larger effect of Berger's novels is to suggest that the novelist's manipulations of the prose surface of his book are those of momentary and isolated control rather than those of ultimate mastery, a state roughly akin to that of a broncobuster who often stays on, but never manages to break, a particular horse. Berger has said that language is "a morality and a politics and a religion" to him, and his novels suggest that indeed in language reside the roots and the power of all such abstract systems.[6] Accordingly, his novels all address the workings of language, particularly the ways in which language determines the perception of reality.

A major assumption underlying Berger's writing would seem to be that our understanding of the referential world is largely determined by the ways we talk about it, the linguistic codes and formulas we have evolved for shaping our lives and our literature. Berger's novels strongly suggest that many of the problems of human existence stem from the reification of verbal constructs and from the consequent confusion of language with the referential world. A corollary implication is that this confusion arises in significant part from the fact that these verbal constructs—linguistic codes for discussing racism, patriotism, or sexuality for instance—are born of efforts to manipulate perceptions of reality for the interest of a particular worldview. Consider that Jack Crabb, in *Little Big Man*, bounces back and forth not just between white and plains Indian cultures but between competing codes of conduct designed to legitimize all manner of cruelty. Berger shows how Jack's greatest problems are at bottom matters of *definition*, and the many different narrative codes Jack employs to tell his story reflect some of the major ways in which we have talked about the West, depending on the moment's perceived needs. Consequently, Berger's novels focus not so much on ideas or themes (although they swell with both) as on the relationship between language and thought. Language *is* Berger's theme, and if his novels can be said to support a central thesis, it is roughly that the interaction of competing and conflicting language codes provides the most important constant of human existence.

Again and again, Berger's novels find new ways to suggest that the structures and institutions that order and give meaning to existence are much less important than the ways we talk about them, and that the ways we talk about those organizing beliefs have inevitably been designed by someone to influence the perception and judgment of someone else. It is in this sense that Berger holds that "fiction is not to be confused with life, because the *latter* is false" (27 June 1976). Berger's novels represent reality as something understood primarily in terms of conflicting and distorting language codes rather than in terms of sensory data, and he also recognizes that his writing of a novel involves him in the creation of one such code or metacode. And just as we have evolved various codes in life for organizing human interchange (codes for meeting, greeting, accusing, winning, losing, etc.), we have evolved innumerable codes for representing human interchange in literature. In virtually every novel, Berger's narrator or characters invoke specific codes, such as the "code of normality" recognized and somewhat ruefully followed by Tony Beeler in *The Feud*. One important function of Berger's formal parataxis is to call attention to the participation of the novel in general, and his novel in particular, in this never-ending attempt to manipulate the understanding of reality. Berger invites his reader to join with him in a consideration of the ways language shapes the perception of reality and of the ways literary codes influence the perception of a novel. Never a polemicist in the usual, narrow sense of the term, Berger tries to reveal in his books both the paradoxes and the possibilities of the ways in which language intersects with immediate experience. A major effect of this effort is that his novels direct our attention toward the situation of our reading as much as, or more than, toward the situations of his characters, while the situations of his characters also raise questions about the role of language codes in our own lives.

Language in the Lives of Berger's Characters

Even a cursory review of Berger's novels reveals that his characters usually find themselves in conflicts that largely result from the vagaries of language: the lives of his characters are affected more by words than by actions, and insofar as true freedom might be defined by Berger as "the ability to be consistent with oneself," his characters are enslaved by language. They are victimized by definitions that exclude or threaten them, by rhetoric that makes them lose sight of physical facts, and by language designed more to preclude than to encourage clear thinking. For this reason, the plot of a Berger novel typically chronicles the efforts of protagonists to free themselves from someone else's verbal version of reality. In this sense, Berger's novels have all explored the processes of *victimization*, with Berger approaching his subject much as a jeweler might examine all of the facets of some bright and terrible diamond. A literary antecedent for this process is not hard to find: no single story could be more emblematic of Berger's concept of victimization than Melville's "Bartleby the Scrivener," a plagiarism of which itself victimizes Carlo Reinhart in *Reinhart in Love*.

From Carlo Reinhart in *Crazy in Berlin* to Lydia Graves in *The Houseguest*, Berger's characters live blurring lives in which they oscillate between being victims and victimizers, between manipulating and being manipulated by the kinds of rhetoric or language codes that organize human life. Reinhart, for instance, knows that his true quest is for "freedom" but also realizes that he cannot "define the nature of his captivity, let alone identify the chief war-

den, though naturally he knew as well as anybody that we are our own jailors"
(172). Berger's protagonists struggle, whether consciously or unconsciously,
to free themselves from the inexorable tendency to think of themselves as victims of outrages and impositions, both humorously small and tragically
large. Almost never in control of the situation around them, these characters
consistently find themselves outmaneuvered, outsmarted, insulted, and imposed upon. Their victimization is usually funny but always serious, often
seemingly trivial but always with an underlying pattern that falls little short
of an old-fashioned naturalistic determinism. While all of his main characters seem on the verge of some momentous discovery that language is all that
really matters, that to control their lives they must first learn to control the
codes that define and evaluate their existence, only Joe Detweiler of *Killing
Time* and Georgie Cornell of *Regiment of Women* seem finally able to break
through the fictions of their verbally determined environments: Detweiler
does so through insanity and Cornell does so through an inadvertent return
to nature.

Berger's characters are wildly dissimilar within each of his books, much
less among them, but just as victimization by language is a constant underlying all of their lives, they do share, to greater or lesser degrees, a single broad
sensibility. Just as Ihab Hassan has termed the protagonist of Berger's
Reinhart series "a custodian of our conscience and of our incongruities,"[7] so
are all of his major characters indeed custodians of conscience and incongruity, rather than architects of a new sensibility or anarchists bent on destroying
the old. Those characters are all observing Ishmaels, acted upon more than
they act, content not so much to try to change or even judge the world around
them as to survive and understand it. Even when granted what might seem to
be fantastic power, as is Fred Wagner in *Being Invisible*, Berger's characters
discover that power can't really change the nature of their lives.

Berger's central, and particularly his peripheral, characters are a string of
outrageously impossible but hauntingly plausible individuals who seem, in
Berger's words, to be "persistent liars" and "monsters of one persuasion or
another."[8] It should be quickly noted that Berger refers to his "monsters" affectionately and within the context of a nonnormative value system. Never
brandable as good or evil, his characters appear to the reader as appealing in
their often bizarre excesses as they are sadly humorous in their deficiencies.
Most important, as Reinhart finally understands of a wife who leaves him
and of a son who taunts and despises him, all of Berger's characters, whether
for good or ill, *do their best*. They may trick, abuse, betray, and even murder
one another, but in a world where understanding seems full of drawbacks and

the irresponsible have, as Reinhart notes, "a permanent one up on those who feel obligations," they are no more and no less than normal.

Whatever Berger's major characters do, they may best be identified by the manner of their thinking. The humorous side of their thinking comes from their desperate fantasies, with which they hopelessly try to forestall disaster, as when in *Who Is Teddy Villanova?* Russel Wren, remembering that he had fenced in college, considers using an old mop to fend off a giant attacker, or when Fred Wagner in *Being Invisible* immediately thinks of throwing his new lover out the window to avoid having her seen by his wife. Whether fantasizing impossible actions or dreaming up outrageous explanations to halt their "thrilling progress towards destruction," Berger's characters inevitably find their dream-logic shattered—usually hilariously —by real life humiliation.

But even in the midst of their desperate fantasies, Berger's characters display a penchant for serious concept spinning or for advancing philosophical propositions. Whether educated or illiterate, young or old, privileged or imposed upon, male or female, his characters are uniformly contemplative, musing about general lessons and principles even when in desperate circumstances. For a Berger character, the attempt to understand experience involves the continuous formation of propositions. These propositions cover aspects of human life both small and large, banal and profound, and often seem a kind of collaboration between Berger's narrators (quite different from book to book) and characters, the former precisely articulating the more vague intuitions, perceptions, and suppositions of the latter. For example, in *The Houseguest,* Bobby Graves's point of view considers the proposition that "the concept of civilized behavior would seem to include a least a sense of balance, if not justice in the narrowest of legalistic senses" (195), while his wife Lydia, who recognizes Bobby's lack of moral strength, feels he may nevertheless make an effective lawyer because "it may well be that the ideal advocate for others is someone who cannot speak effectively for himself—he has no distractions" (8).

Indeed, a more or less steady stream of such propositions identifies its initiating point of view as that of a Berger character, but further discriminations are next to impossible: propositional thinking is what Berger characters have in common, and distinctions among characters rarely emerge from their specific reflections. For example, Earl Keese's observation in *Neighbors* that "anyone who is determined to frustrate an inquiry has an easy time of it: a ridiculous question can be made of every particular of life" (104) could just as easily and naturally have come from Naomi Sandifer in *Sneaky People*—as her proposition that "pornography was a form of farce, inspiring neither ter-

ror nor joy, representing neither aspiration nor achievement, proceeding towards no goal" (279) could have been advanced from his point of view.
Moreover, these propositions stand or fall on their own, their validity or merit
almost never tied to the strengths or weaknesses, virtues or vices, of the character with which they are associated.

In the courtroom of his novels, Berger is neither judge nor advocate, feeling that his job is to maintain his characters in equilibrium, a concern of "art
and not politics or sociology."[9] Accordingly, his novels brim with characters of
wildly opposing viewpoints, none of whom ever has the last word, since
Berger never presents a character whose testimony can be totally believed or
who can be totally discounted. Indeed, those of his characters who most
closely approach straw-man caricature, such as Splendor Mainwaring and
Claude Humbold, prove so consistently outrageous that they are "so chicane
as to achieve finally a kind of integrity."[10] Even an ostensible villain such as
General Custer in *Little Big Man* is not denied the dignity of his conception
of self, even though events reveal the obvious flaws in that conception.

Indeed, all of Berger's characters reflect a fascination with people much
like that ascribed to Reinhart. "Vile they might well be, but it happens that
vileness is fascinating—to a degree of course. For example, he said to himself
now, you will never find a transvestite bear" (338). In many ways, Reinhart
remains the prototypical Berger character, and if he learns any singly most
important lesson during his life, it would seem to be that he must jettison
"the ballast of moral judgment," as he finally realizes that "he had been bur-
dened with it, made lead-footed, hunchbacked, his life long" (VP, 392).

While Reinhart's theory only infrequently coincides with his practice, his
controlling belief is a simple pragmatism that applies to the characters in all
of Berger's novels: "make no mistake, people use us as we ask them to: this is
life's fundamental, and often the only, justice" (CIB, 310).

So persevering is Berger's irony that it not only resists the reader's search
for avuncular social norms but also confronts the reader with a confusing, if
not slightly threatening, mélange of philosophical stances—what might be
thought of as a kind of *thematic* parataxis to reinforce that of Berger's forms.
What critics have been largely unable to see is that Berger characteristically
uses familiar figures in his novels—the chicane businessman, the crooked
politician, the bumbling existential hero—without making them a part of
the familiar assault on the culture of middle America. An editor once told me
that what most intrigued her about Berger was his sense of "social realism,"
precisely what I believe his work does *not* present. That his novels are often
described as satires on society perplexes Berger as much as does the notion
that they are parodies of classic literary forms. "The naive invariably believe

that I strive, and fail, to write social criticism for the delectation of the illiterates who take the daily newspapers seriously and for the semiliterates who make up their staffs. They assume there is a consensus of men of good will and believe that I am trying to associate myself with it" (2 April 1977). Put off by what he refers to as the "platitudes of social meliorism," Berger concerns his fiction more with the perceptual and spiritual foundations of civilization than with its articulation into specific cultures and specific systems of belief. A perversely philosophical blind, German-Jewish, Nazi doctor in *Crazy in Berlin* may suggest Berger's attitude when he warns Reinhart: "If you think I shall tell you what is right or wrong, my friend, you are mistaken. That is your own affair. I care only for practical matters" (341).

Berger's definition of practicality would be something else again, but it is in this vein that Jack Crabb, having bounced back and forth between white and Cheyenne cultures with ample opportunity and inclination to consider the merits of each, finally concludes only that the two approaches to life are different. Frederick Turner has explained how this position is "beyond sentimentality, beyond classic American liberalism," and how, in going beyond literary liberalism, Berger has taken an unusual, if not unique, stance in contemporary American letters.[11] Berger's characters neither represent nor call to mind worthy causes. Instead, they learn, or their lives suggest to the reader, that the very idea of a cause—even one as noble as the code of chivalry Arthur gave to his knights—ultimately works against the best interests of true individuality.

Georgie Cornell, protagonist of *Regiment of Women*, is one of Berger's characters who most directly perceive this to be so: "Everyone he encountered was a monomaniac of some sort, working compulsively to affect someone else: to alter their personality, change their mind, catch them out, set them straight. Everybody else always *knew better* about sex, society, history, you name it—but always in a general way, with absolutely no acknowledgment of one single, particular, individual human being: by which he meant himself" (215).

Most of Berger's main characters share Cornell's suspicion of generalization and also display a general uneasiness about the status of knowledge, most of them explicitly or implicitly understanding the danger in received ideas. In this sense, his characters illustrate one of the central concerns of modernism—the suspicion of certainty—and their lives repeatedly support the wisdom of Gertrude Stein's pronouncement that "knowledge is what *you* know."

Above all, Berger refuses to become another person who *knows better*. As Reinhart once declares in a moment of drunken eloquence: "I'm not here to bury life but to recognize it. If I learned one thing from the sovereign of

Andorra when I served as his medical advisor, it was: Above all, do no harm
and always uphold the dignity of human life. That's as easy, and as hard, to
do whether you're a king or a criminal. So all of you have a good chance"
(RIL, 122).

Reinhart's advice echoes and updates the instructions given David
Copperfield by his aunt—"Never be false, never be mean, never be cruel"—a
credo demanding simpler and clearer vision than Berger's characters can usually muster. Their creator has explained their moral reticence and his own
simply: "the older I get the more reluctant I am to make judgments of that
kind about other people's lives or about all of life. I am happy to say that life
continues to exceed my capacity to define it. And, as Reinhart might say, it
isn't as if one has an alternative."[12]

The Inspiration of Nietzsche

If the description of Berger's philosophical stance sounds somewhat familiar, it is because his novels have much in common with the general view advanced by Nietzsche, particularly in his *Beyond Good and Evil* and *The
Genealogy of Morals*. To note this similarity, however, is far from accounting
for the complicated relationship between Nietzsche's view of the world and
the world of Berger's fiction; Borges's reminder that each writer invents his
precursors may be of special relevance here, a comment anticipated by
Nietzsche's view of reading and readers: "Ultimately, nobody can get more
out of things, including books, than he already knows. For what one lacks access to from experience one will have no ear. . . . Whoever thought he had
understood something of me, had made something out of me after his own
image—not uncommonly an antithesis to me."[13]

What makes the relationship between Berger and Nietzsche so complicated is that Berger's novels tend to be set in worlds that support Nietzsche's
theories of human interchange but do not necessarily lend themselves to
Nietzschean solutions. What Nietzsche describes in a tone always approaching exasperation, Berger portrays with a resigned and often gentle equanimity: the general tenor of his novels is of acceptance rather than of criticism. As
the young Reinhart somewhat fatuously announces to a cynical Berliner: "I
accept life. Some things in it are by nature hateful" (CIB, 378). In Reinhart's
mouth these words are suspect, but if Reinhart's vision is not broad enough
to back such a claim, Berger's is. Berger's comments about Nietzsche make
clear his respect but only begin to hint at the place of Nietzschean thought in
Berger's fiction: "Nietzsche is of the utmost importance to me. I believe that
the wretched era in which he was assumed to be a 'fascist' by idiots who never

opened his work—and for that matter never looked at fascism (else, as idiots, they might well have embraced it)—is at last gone, and nowadays he is simply ignored, as in fact he was ignored in his own day."[14]

Berger approvingly cites Nietzsche's claim in *Beyond Good and Evil* that "there are higher problems than the problems of pleasure and pain and sympathy; and all systems of philosophy which deal only with these are naivetes,"[15] a reference that helps to explain Berger's dissatisfaction with the platitudes of social meliorism, although nowhere in Berger's fiction can be found the championing of suffering with which Nietzsche concludes this discussion. For Nietzsche, the conflict is between the sympathy of the herd and the higher sympathy of the true philosopher or artist. "You want, if possible—and there is not a more foolish "if possible"—*to do away with suffering; and we?*"—it really seems that *we* would rather have it increased and made worse than it has ever been. . . . The discipline of suffering, of *great* suffering—know ye not that it is only *this* discipline that has produced all the elevations of humanity hitherto?"[16] In a letter to Zulfikar Ghose, Berger has glossed this easily misunderstood philosophy: "His vision is utterly original and one cannot understand him unless one puts aside such assumptions as that the poor are necessarily morally superior to the rich or that victims are necessarily heroes. He plunges through such surfaces, rejects such false disjunctions."[17]

Nietzsche's belief that the will to power is the most basic of human motivations and that this will to power has necessarily created morality for selfish reasons and pursued it by immoral ends would seem to be the starting assumption for the world of any Berger novel. "Life," Nietzsche tells us, "is *essentially* appropriation, injury, conquest of the strange and weak, suppression, severity, obtrusion of peculiar forms, and at the least, putting it mildest, exploitation," and a better description of life in the world of Berger's fiction would be hard to find.[18] Nietzsche would seem even to offer a useful explanation for some of the difficulties of Berger's style when he claims, "Every profound spirit needs a mask; nay, more, around every profound spirit there continually grows a mask, owing to the constantly false, that is to say, *superficial* interpretation of every word he utters, every step he takes, every sign of life he manifests."[19]

Berger referred to this discussion of "The Free Spirit" in his 1976 interview with Douglas Hughes, citing in particular Nietzsche's advice: "There are proceedings of such a delicate nature that it is well to overwhelm them with coarseness and make them unrecognizable. I could imagine that a man with something costly and fragile to conceal would roll through life clumsily and rotundly like an old green heavily hooped wine cask, the requirements of his shame requiring it to be so."[20] "That applied to Reinhart," Berger explained, "and Nietzsche continues without a break and what he says applies to me, Reinhart's father: 'A man who has depths in his shame meets his destiny and his delicate decisions upon paths which few ever reach and with regard to the existence of which his nearest and most intimate friends may be ignorant. His mortal danger conceals itself from their eyes and equally so his regained security.'"[21]

And yet, for all the correspondences between Berger's fiction and Nietzsche's philosophy and for all the respect Berger holds for Nietzsche, significant differences appear in the ways in which they proceed from shared assumptions. Perhaps most significant is the disparity between Nietzsche's implication that knowledge can only advance the will to power and Berger's depiction of knowledge as a kind of insidious torment. For Nietzsche knowledge serves to abolish the concept of guilt, but for Berger it is the leading cause of guilt and the necessary precondition for most kinds of suffering—most masochistically, from nothing more than banality. Put another way, the energy that informs so much of Nietzsche's writing can only be seen as ultimately optimistic, while Berger's energy is almost always ironic. One of Reinhart's many epiphanies is that "you can't afford irony if you are seriously interested in acquiring power," and in Berger's novels what Nietzsche would identify as the will to power is always frustrated by a kind of "will to irony," which both enlightens and paralyzes his protagonists.

Berger's sensibility may often coincide with Nietzsche's, but it is not necessarily derived from it. Rather, it seems to me the case that Berger's thinking bears a natural affinity to the antimoralistic, antipietistic stance represented by a number of writers and thinkers—including Nietzsche, Laclos, and Sade—who insist that the official accounts of existence are at best myopic and at worst cynically hypocritical. What must be remembered, however, is that the art of Berger's novels mediates the ideas it may concern itself with. For instance, a Berger character may implicitly or explicitly accept the validity of Nietzsche's account of human interchange without being able to act upon that knowledge. Such a character becomes very ambiguous, since he suggests both that Nietzsche is right and that his being right may not be enough to change anything. As Reinhart laments, "the mere formulation of a principle has absolutely no effect on existence *in re*; which, for example, is why you'll look forever to find a good Christian"(RIL, 87–88). In one ironic sense, the character who understands but cannot profit from Nietzschean thought may be the ultimate victim, the true antithesis to the *Übermensch*, and it is precisely in irony of this sort that Berger most revels. "I never think consciously in a Nietzschean fashion when writing fiction. If I did, I should not be at all

Nietzschean. For me any hint of tendentiousness breaks the fictional trance and one is left with only hateful reality" (26 July 1983).

Like Nietzsche, Berger implicates his reader in the text; like Nietzsche, he views life in dialectical terms; like Nietzsche, he suspects the self-serving pieties of conventional morality; and like Nietzsche, he sees the dangers inherent in the reifying, hypostatizing nature of language. But in Berger's hands these concerns undergo celebration and transformation just as surely as does literary form. In the world of Thomas Berger's fiction, not even Nietzsche has the last word.

Notes and References

Preface

1. Remy de Gourmont, *Selected Writings,* trans. and ed. Glenn S. Burne (Ann Arbor: University of Michigan Press, 1966), 109.
2. *Nowhere* (New York: Delacorte Press/Seymour Lawrence, 1985), 78, 80.
3. Zulfikar Ghose, "Observations from a Correspondence: Letters from Thomas Berger," *Studies in American Humor* 2 (Spring 1983): 11–12.
4. *Who is Teddy Villanova?* (New York: Delacorte Press/Seymour Lawrence, 1977), 8–9. Subsequent page references are to the most recent editions of the novels, identified in the bibliography.

Chapter One

1. Richard Schickel, "Bitter Comedy," *Commentary,* July 1970, 80.
2. Alan Wilde, "Acts of Definition, or Who Is Thomas Berger?," *Arizona Quarterly* 39 (Winter 1983):314–315.
3. Richard Ohmann, "The Shaping of a Canon: U. S. Fiction, 1960–1975," in *Canons,* ed. Robert von Hallberg (Chicago: University of Chicago Press, 1984), 392–94.
4. Schickel, "Bitter Comedy," 77.
5. Ghose, "Observations," 11–12.
6. Schickel, "Bitter Comedy," 77.
7. Thomas R. Edwards, "Domestic Guerrillas," *New York Times Book Review,* 6 April 1980, 1.
8. Leonard Michaels, "If Hammett and Chandler Were Written by Perelman: *Who Is Teddy Villanova?*," New York Times Book Review, 20 March 1977, 1.
9. Berger remarked to me in a letter of 27 June 1976, "Remember that you will understand my work best when you are at your most selfish."
10. Burroughs Mitchell, *The Education of an Editor* (New York: Doubleday, 1980), 142.
11. Wilde, "Acts of Definition," 341.
12. Thomas Berger, response in "Who Created Whom? Characters That Talk Back," *New York Times Book Review,* 31 May 1987, 36.
13. Michael Malone, "Berger, Burlesque, and the Yearning for Comedy," *Studies in American Humor* 2 (Spring 1983): 21.
14. Douglas Hughes, "Thomas Berger's Elan: An Interview," *Confrontation* 12 (Summer 1976): 24.

15. Ghose, "Observations," 8.

16. Hughes, "Elan," 37.

17. Referred to as "a brilliant paper" in Berger's 1951 *Intro* review, "Orwell as Essayist; Pound as Correspondent," this essay appears in Lionel Trilling, *The Liberal Imagination* (New York: Doubleday, 1950.

18. Hughes, "Elan," 24.

19. Richard Schickel, "Interviewing Thomas Berger," *New York Times Book Review,* 6 April 1980, 22.

Chapter Two

1. R. V. Cassill, "Reinhart Back from Berlin, Out of Love and Ready for Freezing," *New York Times Book Review,* 29 March 1970, 4.

2. Hughes, "Elan," 33.

3. Ihab Hassan, "Conscience and Incongruity: The Fiction of Thomas Berger," *Critique: Studies in Modern Fiction* 5, no. 2 (1962): 4.

4. Douglas Hughes, "The Schlemiel as Humanist: Thomas Berger's Carlo Reinhart," *Cithara* 15, no. 1 (1975):7.

5. Gerald Weales, "Reinhart as Hero and Clown," *Hollins Critic* 20 (December 1983): 2.

6. Ibid.

7. Berger, response in "Who Created Whom?," 36.

8. Wilde, "Acts of Definition," 341.

9. Apart from the previously cited articles by Hassan, Hughes, and Wilde, the series has been the focus of the seminal review-essay by Schickel, "Bitter Comedy," and of essays by Sanford Pinsker, "The World according to Carl Reinhart: Thomas Berger's Comic Vision"; Ronald R. Janssen, "The Voice of Our Culture: Thomas Berger's Reinhart in Love"; and Myron Simon, "*Crazy in Berlin* as Ethnic Comedy"—all of which appeared in the two-volume "Special Issue Honoring Thomas Berger," *Studies in American Humor* 2, nos. 1 and 2 (Spring and Fall 1983).

10. Steve Paul, "Thomas Berger Yields to Comic-Writer Image," *Kansas City Star,* 30 March 1986, 9J.

11. Harvey Swados, "An American in Berlin," *New Leader,* 15 December 1958, 24.

12. Weales, "Hero and Clown," 4.

13. Hughes, "Elan," 28.

14. Jonathan Baumbach, review of *Reinhart's Women, American Book Review,* 20 March 1982, 16.

15. Jean Moore, "Author of *Neighbors* Says It's His Favorite," *Tampa Tribune,* 21 December 1981, 6D.

Chapter Three

1. Hughes, "Elan," 31–32.

2. L. L. Lee, "American, Western, Picaresque: Thomas Berger's *Little Big Man*," *South Dakota Review*, 4, no. 2 (1966): 35–42.

3. Frederick W. Turner III, "The Second Decade of *Little Big Man*," *Nation*, 20–27 August 1977, 149.

4. Edward Adamson Hoebel, *The Cheyennes: Indians of the Great Plains* (New York: Holt, 1960), 99.

5. Ibid., 64–66.

6. George Bird Grinnell, *The Fighting Cheyennes* (Norman: University of Oklahoma Press, 1956), 13–17.

7. Ibid., 119.

8. Frank B. Linderman, *Plenty-Coups: Chief of the Crows* (Lincoln: University of Nebraska Press, 1962), 98.

9. Francis Parkman, *The Oregon Trail*, ed. E. N. Felskog (Madison: University of Wisconsin Press, 1969), 204–211.

10. Turner, "Second Decade," 150.

11. Leo E. Oliva, "Thomas Berger's *Little Big Man* as History," *Western American Literature* 8 (1973) :33–54.

12. Henry Nash Smith, *Virgin Land: The American West as Symbol and Myth* (Cambridge: Harvard University Press, 1973), 90–111.

13. Turner, "Second Decade," 150.

14. Walter Blair, *Native American Humor* (Scranton, Pa: Chandler, 1960), 91.

15. Ibid., 87.

16. Richard Bridgman, *The Colloquial Style in America* (New York: Oxford University Press, 1966), 144.

17. Evan S. Connell, *Son of the Morning Star* (San Francisco: North Point, 1984), 301. With every page Connell's fine study of Custer and the Battle of the Little Bighorn confirms Berger's research, instinct, and imagination in *Little Big Man*.

18. Thomas Berger, afterword to *The Pathfinder*, by James Fenimore Cooper (New York: New American Library, 1961), 432.

19. Daniel Royot, "Aspects of the American Picaresque in *Little Big Man*," in *Les Americanistes: New French Criticism on Modern American Fiction*, ed. Ira D. Johnson and Christiane Johnson (Port Washington, N.Y.: Kennikat Press, 1978): 43.

20. Berger, afterword, 432.

21. Frederick W. Turner III, "Melville and Thomas Berger: The Novelist as Cultural Anthropologist," *Centennial Review* 13 (1969): 101–21.

22. Royot, "Aspects of the American Picaresque," 42–43.

23. Berger, afterword, 435.

24. Smith, *Virgin Land*, 101.

Chapter Four

1. Hughes, "Elan," 34.

2. Garrett Epps, Review of *Arthur Rex,* by Thomas Berger, *New Republic,* 7 October 1978, 34.

3. Michael Malone, "Berger, Burlesque, and the Yearning for Comedy," *Studies in American Humor* 2 (Spring 1983): 24.

4. Thomas Berger, foreward to *German Medieval Tales,* ed. Francis G. Gentry (New York: Continuum, 1983), viii.

5. Some ten years after making this remark, Berger clarified that in calling children "naturally vicious," he was calling them "not evil but human." He concluded, "I am not a Rousseauist: I do not believe that man is born either free or innocent" (7 August 1987).

6. Eugene Vinaver, ed., *King Arthur and His Knights: Selected Tales by Sir Thomas Malory* (New York: Oxford University Press, 1975), xiii.

7. Charles Moorman, *The Book of Kyng Arthur: The Unity of Malory's "Morte Darthur"* (Lexington: University of Kentucky Press, 1965).

8. Suggesting even deeper links between *Arthur Rex* and *Little Big Man,* Michael Malone—one of the handful of first-rate commentators on Berger's writing—has noted the metaphorical importance of the circle to both works, and in each case the circle becomes an emblem of antihierarchical thinking. Malone, "Berger, Burlesque," 28.

9. John Romano, "Camelot and All That," *New York Times Book Review,* 12 November 1978, 62. A recent analysis of contemporary Arthurian literature, Raymond H. Thompson's *The Return From Avalon: A Study of the Arthurian Legend in Modern Fiction* (Westport Conn.: Greenwood, 1985), 155, found Berger's work "in many ways the most impressive" modern Arthurian ironic fantasy.

Chapter Five

1. Samuel Butler, *Erewhon* (New York: Lancer, 1968), 16.

2. Quentin Reynolds, *Courtroom* (Garden City, N.Y.: Garden City Books, 1951); Fredric Wertham, *The Show of Violence* (Garden City, N.Y.: Doubleday and Co., 1949). Berger literally stepped on a copy of the Reynolds book in the parking lot of the Grand Union supermarket in Nyack, New York, in the early 1960s. "My foot felt an object on the asphalt. I looked down: it was a wretched paperback, swollen fat from rainsoak and subsequent drying. I knew before looking at the title that the Muse had left it there for me. It was Quentin Reynolds' *Courtroom.* The only useful thing that I can say beyond that is I quite seriously believe that whatever God said to Robert Irwin, He really did tell Joe Detweiler to kill those terrible people" (18 March 1979).

3. Thomas Berger, "Films," *Esquire,* April 1972, 30.

4. Hughes, "Elan," 36.

5. Richard Todd, "God's First Mistakes," *Atlantic,* September 1973, 106.

6. These reviews often acknowledged that *Regiment of Women,* was "puzzling" or "difficult," some going so far as to ascribe their confusion to Berger by suggesting that he had not been sure of his intent.

7. Lore Dickstein, review of *Regiment of Women*, by Thomas Berger, *Ms.,* August 1973, 33.

8. Ibid. Elizabeth Stone, one of the few other women to review the book, reached an almost identical conclusion in her review of *Regiment of Women,* by Thomas Berger, *Crawdaddy,* October 1973, 89–90.

9. Leo Braudy, review of *Regiment of Women*, by Thomas Berger, *New York Times Book Review,* 13 May 1973, 6. Braudy sums up his praise for the novel by stating that it "has been imagined with such ferocity and glee that we assent to it almost in spite of ourselves, celebrating with Berger that anarchic individuality that outlasts all the forms that language and society attempt to impose upon it."

10. Walter Clemons, "Georgie's Travels," *Newsweek,* 21 May 1973, 102.

11. Braudy, review of *Regiment of Women,* 6.

12. Gertrude Stein, *The Geographical History of America or the Relation of Human Nature to the Human Mind* (New York: Vintage, 1975), 122.

13. Ghose, "Observations," 11–12.

Chapter Six

1. See, for example, Stanley Trachtenberg, "Invisible Men," *Chicago Tribune,* 12 April 1987, sec. 14, p. 7.

2. Francine Prose, "Outnumbered by Jerks," 9.

3. Hughes, "Elan," 31.

4. D. Keith Mano, review of *Sneaky People,* "A Good Book by a Good Writer, Thomas Berger," *New York Times Book Review,* 20 April 1975, 4. Mano's review opens: "What you do, see, is go out and buy *Sneaky People.* Period. No questions asked."

5. Hughes, "Elan," 36–37.

6. Ibid.

7. McDowell, "Publishing: Pulitzer Controversies," *New York Times,* 11 May 1984, 26.

8. Schickel, "Interviewing Thomas Berger," 21.

9. Friedrich Nietzsche, *The Dawn,* sec. 113, cited by Walter Kaufmann, *Nietzsche: Philosopher, Psychologist, Antichrist* (New York: Meridian Books, 1965), 168. I am indebted to Stephen P. Thompson for calling to my attention some of the remarkably specific parallels in *Neighbors* to Nietzsche's *Beyond Good and Evil* and *The Genealogy of Morals.*

10. Schickel, "Interviewing Thomas Berger," 21.

Chapter Seven

1. Roland Barthes, "To Write: An Intransitive Verb?," in *The Language of*

Criticism and the Sciences of Man, ed. R. Macksey and E. Donato (Baltimore: Johns Hopkins University Press, 1970), 144.

2. Schickel, "Interviewing Thomas Berger," 21.

3. E. H. Gombrich, *Art and Illusion* (Princeton: Princeton University Press, 1960), 244.

4. Hughes, "Elan," 31.

5. John Leonard, "Books of the Times," *New York Times,* 18 March 1977, C21.

6. Hughes, "Elan," 27.

7. Ihab Hassan, "Conscience and Incongruity," 4.

8. Hughes, "Elan," 33.

9. Ibid., 33.

10. Ibid., 31.

11. Turner, "The Second Decade," 150.

12. Hughes, "Elan," 28.

13. Friedrich Nietzsche, "Why I Write Such Good Books," in *Ecce Homo,* ed. Walter Kaufmann (New York: Vintage, 1967), 261.

14. Hughes, "Elan," 28.

15. Ibid.

16 Friedrich Nietzsche, *Beyond Good and Evil,* vol. 12 of *The Complete Works,* ed. Oscar Levy (New York: Russell & Russell, 1964), 170–171.

17. Ghose, "Observations," 15.

18. Nietzsche, *Beyond Good and Evil,* 226.

19. Ibid., 56.

20. Hughes, "Elan," 29.

21. Ibid., 29.

Selected Bibliography

For information about Berger's numerous other short writings, and additional reviews and critical essays about his work, readers should consult James Bense, "Works by and about Thomas Berger," *Studies in American Humor* 2 (Fall 1983): 142–52.

PRIMARY WORKS

Books

Arthur Rex: A Legendary Novel. New York: Delacorte Press/Seymour Lawrence, 1978. Reprint. New York: Laurel/Seymour Lawrence, 1985 (paperback).

Being Invisible. New York: Little, Brown & Co., 1987. Reprint. New York: Penguin, 1988 (paperback).

Crazy in Berlin. New York: Charles Scribner's Sons, 1958. Reprint. New York: Delta/Seymour Lawrence, 1982 (paperback).

The Feud. New York: Delacorte Press/Seymour Lawrence, 1983. Reprint. New York: Delta/Seymour Lawrence, 1984 (paperback).

Granted Wishes: Three Stories. Northridge, Calif.: Lord John Press, 1984. (Originally published in *Harper's,* October 1982, 52–59.)

The Houseguest. New York: Little, Brown & Co. 1988. Reprint. New York: Penguin, 1989 (paperback).

Killing Time. New York: Dial Press, 1967. Reprint. New York: Delta/Seymour Lawrence, 1981 (paperpack).

Little Big Man. New York: Dial Press, 1964. Reprint. New York: Laurel/Seymour Lawrence, 1985 (paperback).

Neighbors. New York: Delacorte Press/Seymour Lawrence, 1980. Reprint. New York: Delta/Seymour Lawrence, 1981 (paperback).

Nowhere. New York: Delacorte Press/Seymour Lawrence, 1985. Reprint. New York: Delta/Seymour Lawrence, 1986 (paperback).

Regiment of Women. New York: Simon and Schuster, 1973. Reprint. New York: Delta/Seymour Lawrence, 1982 (paperback).

Reinhart in Love. New York: Charles Scribner's Sons, 1962. Reprint. New York: Delta/Seymour Lawrence, 1982 (paperback).

Reinhart's Women. New York: Delacorte Press/Seymour Lawrence, 1981. Reprint. New York: Delta/Seymour Lawrence, 1982 (paperback).

Sneaky People. New York: Simon and Schuster, 1975. Reprint. New York: Delta/Seymour Lawrence, 1983 (paperback).

Vital Parts. New York: Richard W. Baron, 1970. Reprint. New York: Delta/Seymour Lawrence, 1982 (paperback).

Who Is Teddy Villanova? New York: Delacorte Press/Seymour Lawrence, 1977. Reprint. New York: Delta/Seymour Lawrence, 1978 (paperback).

Other Writing

"A Statement." In *Dictionary of Literary Biography Yearbook: 1980,* edited by
Karen L. Rood, Jean W. Ross, and Richard Ziegfeld, 17. Detroit: Gale Re-
search Co., 1981.
Other People, act 1. In *Works in Progress,* no. 6, 45–75. New York: Literary Guild of
America, 1972.
Afterword to *The Pathfinder,* by James Fenimore Cooper, 429–38. New York: New
American Library, 1961.
Foreword to *German Medieval Tales,* edited by Francis G. Gentry, vii–x. New York:
Continuum, 1983.

SECONDARY WORKS

Interviews and Letters

Ghose, Zulfikar. "Observations from a Correspondence: Letters from Thomas
Berger." *Studies in American Humor* 2 (Spring 1983): 5–19. Illuminating ex-
cerpts from a twenty-year correspondence with writer, critic, and friend
Zulfikar Ghose.
Hughes, Douglas. "Thomas Berger's Elan: An Interview." *Confrontation,* no. 12
(1976): 23–39. By far the most extensive and useful Berger interview.
Schickel, Richard. "Interviewing Thomas Berger." *New York Times Book Review,* 6
April 1980. Focuses on *Neighbors* and offers a valuable update to the Hughes
interview.

General Overviews of Berger's Writing

Landon, Brooks. "The Radical Americanist." *Nation,* 20–27 August 1977, 151–
153. Praise for Berger's first eight novels; suggests that reading his celebrations
of fictional forms is unsettling "since his oblique assaults on popular concep-
tions of rationality never advertise their complexity, while his experiments never
parade themselves as such."
Malone, Michael. "Berger, Burlesque, and the Yearning for Comedy." *Studies in
American Humor* 2 (Spring 1983): 20–32. A persuasive analysis of Berger's
complexity that also considers why his achievements have not been better celebrated. Whatever the novel form, Berger writes comedy, as opposed to comic
novels, bringing us, as does Beckett, "to confront our *metaphysical* (as opposed
to our social) bewilderment."
Moore, Jean P. "Thomas Berger's 'Joyful Worship': A Study of Form and Parody."
Studies in American Humor 2 (Spring 1983): 72–82. Berger's writing reveals
his postmodern sensibility, but its most significant feature is "the revitalizing of
received forms through the innovative, creative use of their conventions." Form
and language are foregrounded in Berger's novels, "pointing out the fictive na-

ture of his art," not reflecting "meaning inherent in the world," but creating meaning, implying distinctions between art and truth. Essay reflects thesis of Moore's dissertation on Berger.

Wilde, Alan. "Acts of Definition, or Who Is Thomas Berger?" *Arizona Quarterly* 39 (Winter 1983): 314–15. (Republished in Alan Wilde, *Middle Grounds: Studies in Contemporary American Fiction*. Philadelphia: University of Pennsylvania Press, 1987. This is perhaps the singly most instructive essay on Berger's work, indispensable scholarship even though I disagree with several of its conclusions. Wilde's phenomenology of Berger astutely recognizes the inseparability for the author of the concepts of freedom and of self definition, but finds in Berger's novels a "fear of otherness" which I would instead call "fascination."

Articles and Major Reviews Focused on Individual Novels

Cassill, R. V. "Reinhart Back from Berlin, Out of Love and Ready for Freezing." *New York Times Book Review*, 29 March 1970. Excellent assessment of first three Reinhart books.

Dickstein, Lore. Review of *Regiment of Women*, by Thomas Berger. *Ms.*, August 1973, 32–34. Evenhanded feminist review.

Edwards, Thomas R. "Domestic Guerrillas." *New York Times Book Review*, 6 April 1980. Review of *Neighbors* makes a strong case for Berger's importance in American literature, calling our failure to read and study Berger "a national disgrace."

Grace, Sherrill E. "Western Myths and Northern History." *Great Plains Quarterly* 3 (Summer 1983): 146–56. An excellent discussion of Jack Crabb as a "genuine fabulator," a character "who knows how to exploit and manipulate language and rhetorical style." Jack's self-consciously crafted story is twentieth century captivity narrative that "explores all the white psychological fears and taboos" of early captivity narratives, "while at the same time exploiting the ritual and mythic pattern of all such narratives."

Gurian, Jay. "Style in the Literary Desert: *Little Big Man*." *Western American Literature* 3 (1969): 285–96. Noting that Berger "never sacrifices his imagination to realism," Gurian argues that *Little Big Man* "is a great novel because it portrays western 'society' in the nineteenth century as it really was—violent, yes, but also absurd, melodramatic, incongruous."

Hassan, Ihab. "Conscience and Incongruity: The Fiction of Thomas Berger." *Critique: Studies in Modern Fiction* 5, no. 2 (1962): 4–15. The first critical acknowledgment of Berger's complexity in *Crazy in Berlin* and *Reinhart in Love*.

Hughes, Douglas A. "The Schlemiel as Humanist: Thomas Berger's Carlo Reinhart." *Cithara* 15, no. 1 (1975): 3–21. An insightful reading of the first three Reinhart books. Reinhart, "an embodiment of those humanist values the author wishes to celebrate," clearly belongs in the tradition of the Jewish schlemiel-hero, the wise fool whose very real shortcomings are mitigated by his essential goodness."

Janssen, Ronald R. "The Voice of Our Culture: Thomas Berger's *Reinhart in Love. Studies in American Humor* 2 (Fall 1983): 111-16. This essay by the first scholar to write a doctoral dissertation on Berger locates the novel's comedy in the inspection and criticism of "the values expressed in American material culture, especially as those values are promulgated by and through American commerce."

Lee, L. L. "American, Western, Picaresque: Thomas Berger's *Little Big Man.*" *South Dakota Review* 4, no. 2 (1966): 35–42. The picaresque form of *Little Big Man* allows the author to explore western myth without becoming its sentimental victim. Berger's theme is that "the truly worthy man is the individual," meaning "to have the courage and strength to live one's own life."

Madden, David. "Thomas Berger's Comic-Absurd Vision in *Who is Teddy Villanova?*" *Armchair Detective* 14 (1981): 37–43. Compares TV with Chandler's *Farewell, My Lovely;* unlike Chandler, Berger has his protagonist expose not hidden truth, but the elusiveness of truth.

Malone, Michael. "American Literature's *Little Big Man.*" *Nation* 3 May 1980: 535–37. An important review essay, describing *Neighbors* as a "flawlessly crafted morality play," and judging Berger "the real thing: a major Major Writer." After stating the "no one at work in this country writes better than he does—and precious few write anywhere near as well," Malone explains some of the reasons for Berger's relative lack of fame. He identifies Berger's three basic themes as a "war with time," a "yearning for human rightness," and "a baffled love of women in uneasy tension with idealistic aspirations about manliness and realistic despair about sexual politics."

Mano, D. Keith. "A Good Book by a Good Writer, Thomas Berger." *New York Times Book Review,* 20 April 1975, 4–5. Exuberantly perceptive review of *Sneaky People,* with special attention to the style of its narrative.

Oliva, Leo E. "Thomas Berger's *Little Big Man* as History." *Western American Literature* 8 (1973): 33–54. Thoroughly documents the historical accuracy of details in *Little Big Man* (finding only one chronological incongruity), while praising the creative skill with which Berger assembled those details.

Romano, John. "Camelot and All That." *New York Times Book Review,* 12 November 1978. Review of *Arthur Rex* in which Romano identifies as the wry paradox at the book's heart the belief that "doing good in a world that is mostly bad can have bizarre or disastrous consequences." Praises Berger's power "to be both farcical and moving at once" and concludes that *Arthur Rex* is "the Arthur book for our time."

Royot, Daniel. "Aspects of the American Picaresque in *Little Big Man.*" In *Les Americanistes: New French Criticism on Modern American Fiction,* edited by Ira D. Johnson and Christiane Johnson, 37–52. Port Washington, N. Y.: Kennikat Press, 1978. French concepts of the picaresque need to be modified to understand how "Crabb's unique experience withstands efforts toward generalization," and how his adventures "teach that reality is at best seen as someone's make-believe."

Schickel, Richard. "Bitter Comedy." *Commentary,* July 1970, 76–80. This review of *Vital Parts* offers an astute introduction to Berger's writing, positing his theme as "the devastation of the individualist ethic by the spirit of our time," and specifying Berger's basic belief that "as we lose faith in our traditional individualism we seek, at every level of life, compensatory fantasies of power, of escape, of impractical idealism." Schickel was one of the first critics to recognize Berger's uniqueness, and he remains one of the most able commentators on Berger's writing.

Swados, Harvey. "An American in Berlin." *New Leader,* 15 December 1958, 24. Unusually perceptive review of *Crazy in Berlin* by a fellow novelist.

Thompson, Raymond H. *The Return from Avalon: A Study of the Arthurian Legend in Modern Fiction.* Westport, Conn.: Greenwood, 1985. See pages 155–61. *Arthur Rex* is "in many ways the most impressive" of contemporary Arthurian ironic fantasies.

Turner III, Frederick W. "Melville and Thomas Berger: The Novelist as Cultural Anthropologist." *Centennial Review* 13 (1969): 101–21. Compares the project of *Little Big Man* with that of Melville's *Israel Potter.*

———. "The Second Decade of *Little Big Man*," *Nation,* 20–27 August 1977, 149–151. Celebrates *Little Big Man* as a "seminal event in what must now seem the most significant cultural and literary trend of the last decade: the attempt on many fronts to develop structures, styles, ways of thinking that are beyond any version of ethnocentrism."

Wallace, Jon. "A Murderous Clarity: An Intertextual Reading of Thomas Berger's *Killing Time.*" *Philological Quarterly.* In press. Superb analysis of philosophical implications of Berger's use of sources in *Killing Time.*

———. "The Implied Author as Protagonist: A Reading of *Little Big Man. Western American Literature* 22 (February 1988): 291–99. Excellent focus on the form of *Little Big Man.* By attending to the implied author behind Snell and Crabb, "we discover not only another voice in Berger's novel . . . but also another story that is told in terms of style rather than plot."

Weales, Gerald. "Reinhart as Hero and Clown." *Hollins Critic* 20 (December 1983): 1–12. "The strength of the Reinhart books is that the reader keeps recognizing his similarities to the good fool, the horse's ass, when he would prefer to identify with the poet-philosopher hero that Reinhart spends so many years imagining hidden within his untidy mind and body."

Weber, Brom. "The mode of 'Black Humor.'" In *The Comic Imagination in American Literature,* edited by Louis D. Rubin, Jr., 361–71. New Brunswick, N.J.: Rutgers University Press, 1973. Identifies Berger as one of the few writers who have escaped the "decline in quality and prestige" of the longstanding American black humor tradition." Places *Vital Parts* "in the great black humor tradition of Hawthorne, Melville, Faulkner."

Index